KU-462-761

FREUD'S *PROJECT* REASSESSED

KARL H. PRIBRAM
MERTON M. GILL

FREUD'S *PROJECT* REASSESSED

HUTCHINSON OF LONDON

Hutchinson & Co (Publishers) Ltd
3 Fitzroy Square, London W1

London Melbourne Sydney Auckland
Wellington Johannesburg and agencies
throughout the world

First published 1976
© Karl H. Pribram and Merton Gill 1976

Set in Monotype Baskerville
Printed in Great Britain by The Anchor Press Ltd
and bound by Wm Brendon & Son Ltd
both of Tiptree, Essex

ISBN 0 09 124980 5

For some months in the year 1895 Sigmund Freud was seized by a creative spell in which he tried to systematize his basic ideas of the functioning of the human mind, in particular of its neuropsychological mechanisms. He wrote out his views and sent the manuscript to his friend Wilhelm Fliess, to which circumstance we owe its preservation, for it was not published till posthumously in 1950.

Though Freud gave the manuscript no title he had referred to it in a letter to Fliess as the 'Psychology for Neurologists'. The editor of the English translation named it the 'Project for a Scientific Psychology' and it is usually referred to by psychoanalysts as the *Project*, the name we use in the title of our book.

Its importance lies in the fact that it contains explicit formulations and definitions of many central concepts and terms of that branch of psychoanalytic theory known as metapsychology, concepts and terms that Freud continued to use throughout his life but never again defined as explicitly and comprehensively.

We have the remarkable situation then that these important definitions and formulations are to be found in their clearest form in an early unpublished work. Our purpose is to use these explicit formulations to clarify much that is otherwise obscure in the received metapsychology, and thus to illuminate its relationship to contemporary cognitive theory and neuropsychology.

CONTENTS

PROLOGUE

During the 1960s psychology experienced a revolution. Trends of half a century were sharply reversed and issues that had been ignored during this period suddenly re-emerged full force. Behaviouristic procedure had lost touch with the intrapsychic world that feeds most people's interest in the field. The revolutionary turn was that academic experimental psychology, which had become comfortably operational and functional in its behaviourism, turned cognitive, structural, intentional, and subjective.

Yet in the clinical realm behaviourism resulted in the development of what is now the influential field of behaviour therapy. One may perhaps debate whether in fact the principles which gave rise to behaviour therapy actually operate to produce its results, but it is clear that academic cognitive psychology has as yet failed to venture *any* clinically relevant theory.

Our concern in the present work is with the development of a cognitive and control theory which could become clinically relevant. Academic cognitive psychology has dealt with verbal coding, with pattern recognition, with control processes such as attention and intentional performance, and with the organization of memory and thought. The insights obtained provide a wealth of principles to be applied to clinical problems.

However, an important problem must be faced in making such applications. Whereas behaviouristic psychology had an apparently clear theoretical field in which to develop its clinical applications, cognitive scientists will find in classical psychoanalysis and all of its offshoots a venerable psychology formulated on its own terms. Unfortunately, the formulation includes large segments (the meta-

9

psychology, see below) that appear to be couched in pronouncement rather than observation and experimentation. This criticism does not deny the spirit of inquiry which has always characterized psychoanalysis. We refer rather to its relative isolation from contemporary scientific procedure and data.

Quite separately, coming from different disciplines, we found what we believe to be a way to deal with these problems. Our way proposes no completely new approach but rather returns to the roots of the problem. As we shall see, we agree with those who distinguish two bodies of cognitive formulations in psychoanalysis – the clinical theory and the metapsychology. Clinical theory, better labelled 'psychology' (though Freud originally used the term psychology for what is now called metapsychology), encompasses those formulations derived from observations in the analytic situation and stated in the intentional language of motivations and meanings; while metapsychology describes the *mechanisms* of such mental functioning. In contemporary psychoanalysis, the clinical and metapsychological formulations have often become confused, and Gill (1976) has urged their separation elsewhere. We make a beginning in disentangling these confusions in this monograph by an exploration of the roots of the metapsychology.

Our analysis shows that Freud initially formulated the mechanisms of mental function on the basis of his biological and neurological knowledge. He then chose, for a variety of reasons, to leave these neurobiological foundations implicit – indeed on occasion to deny their existence. Nevertheless he kept the mechanisms basically intact. But deprived of their roots and explicitness, the mechanisms became isolated from contemporary developments in science and, especially in the hands of post-Freudian psychoanalysts, became elaborated into a speculative tangle of concepts and casuistry. Thus when we came across the original formulations, published posthumously as the *Project for a Scientific Psychology*, we felt marvellously refreshed. Opacities and conceptualizations that had defied analysis were clarified and, most importantly, these conceptualizations were seen tied to the then existing body of scientific knowledge and not arising *de novo* from Freud's fertile imagination. The concrete neurobiological hypotheses in the *Project* are subject to testing and modification in the light of new findings and alternate conceptualizations.

So we took on the job of re-viewing the *Project* in order to display the roots of metapsychology and to reappraise them. We argue that the metapsychology is a neuropsychology that can be modified in terms of current neurophysiology; that the regulatory principles are better understood by reference to the advances in information, control, and systems theory; that the formulations of memory-motive mechanisms, attention, consciousness, and thought processes are as sophisticated as any available elsewhere and should therefore become part of the heritage of academic cognitive psychology.

Important roots of the clinical theory lie in the *Project* also. We consider some of them in our chapter on associative and dissociative processes in dreams and psychopathology. However, these clinical formulations are not the major preoccupation of this monograph though they continue to be basic and pervasive in the development of psychoanalysis.

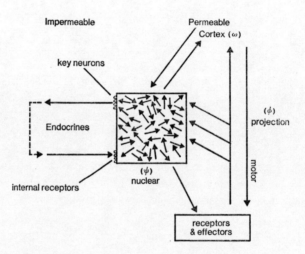

Stylized representation of the 'machine' or 'model' of psychological processes presented in the *Project*.

One evening last week when I was hard at work, tormented with just that amount of pain that seems to be the best state to make my brain function, the barriers were suddenly lifted, the veil was drawn aside, and I had a clear vision from the details of the neuroses to the conditions that make consciousness possible. Everything seemed to connect up, the whole worked well together, and one had the impression that the thing was now really a machine and would soon go by itself. The three systems of neurones, the free and bound state of Quantity, the primary and secondary processes, the main tendency and the compromise tendency of the nervous system, the two biological laws of attention and defence, the indications of Quality, Reality, and Thought, the (particular) position of the psychosexual group, the sexual determinant of repression, and finally the necessary conditions for consciousness as a function of perception: all that was perfectly clear, and still is. Naturally, I don't know how to contain myself for pleasure.

(Freud, Letter to Wilhelm Fliess,
20 October, 1895,
S.E., vol. 1, p. 285)

INTRODUCTION

Our encounters with Freud's *Project for a Scientific Psychology*, his 'Psychology for Neurologists', have been filled with the same sense of surprise and excitement which Freud so movingly expressed in his letters to Fliess – and wonder that the 'thing' could really 'go by itself'. For, despite our different disciplinary backgrounds, we found that 'everything seemed to connect up', that 'the whole worked well together'. This enthusiasm for the *Project* has not left us in the decade and a half since we initially became involved with it.

Our purpose here is to show that psychoanalytic metapsychology should be seen to be in all its facets a biological cognitive control theory, based on an explicit neuropsychology. Our initial attempts to transmit our views to others interested in psychology and psychiatry produced a manuscript which a friend astutely labelled 'A very long book review, and not a very critical one at that'. The problem was that most readers felt that, despite evidence to the contrary, we had *interpreted* Freud when in *fact* we were quoting him. We concluded that few really care what Freud actually said in 1895, no matter how insightful he might have been for the time in which he lived. What our audience repeatedly asked was, 'What do *you* think of it on the basis of current knowledge; how is this relevant to *our* interests, here and now?'

Yet our conviction was and is that what Freud wrote in 1895 *is* important and needs exposition. We disagree with the commonly stated view that the *Project* is an ostensibly neurological document but really a psychological one cloaked in neurological terms and that Freud had the courage later to shed the neurological cloak of metapsychology. Nor do we believe the reverse, that the *Project* is, as Kanzer (1973) would have it, manifestly an essentially psychological document.

14

We believe that the *Project* is in the main a neuropsychologic document in which, as Kanzer in the same article sharply points out, the point of departure for the neuropsychological hypotheses often is a psychological observation, though, as Kanzer seems less clearly to recognize, it is also sometimes a neurological hypothesis. We also believe that the later metapsychology is ostensibly psychological alone but is in fact neuropsychology, with the neurology rendered implicit in contrast to its explicit statement in the *Project*.

As Strachey (S.E., vol. 1, p. 290) wrote: '. . . in fact the *Project*, or rather its invisible ghost, haunts the whole series of Freud's theoretical writings to the very end.'

And again Strachey (Introduction to *The Interpretation of Dreams*) says:

It is no exaggeration to say that much of the seventh chapter of *The Interpretation of Dreams*, and, indeed, of Freud's later 'metapsychological' studies, has only become fully intelligible since the publication of the *Project*. Students of Freud's theoretical writings have been aware that even in his profoundest psychological speculations little or no discussion is to be found upon some of the *most* fundamental of the concepts of which he makes use: such concepts, for instance, as 'mental energy', 'sums of excitation', 'cathexis', 'quantity', 'quality', 'intensity', and so on. . . . The paucity of explanation of such basic notions in Freud's later writings suggests that he was taking it for granted that they were as much a matter of course to his readers as they were to himself; and we owe it as a debt of gratitude to the posthumously published correspondence with Fliess that it throws so much light precisely upon these obscurities.

(S.E., vol. 4, pp. xv–xvi)

But these are not the only psychoanalytic concepts which find their first major systematic exposition in the *Project* and are illuminated by it. For the *Project* also not only introduces but also suggests neurobiological mechanisms for such major psychoanalytic concepts as the primary and secondary processes, the ego, reality testing, drive, and defence. While these concepts are also developed in later writings on essentially psychological grounds, the *Project* reveals some of the hidden neurobiological assumptions with which they remained intertwined. We believe that even their clarification on psychological grounds alone is illuminated by revealing these implicit assumptions.

But even that is not all. The *Project* contains a detailed motivational theory of thinking and an equally detailed theory of consciousness, the latter resting on explicit formulations of the mechanism of attention.

These contributions should rank with Freud's monograph *On Aphasia* (1891), reviewed by Otto M. Marx (1970), as classic contributions that continue to be pertinent to the contemporary wide interest of psychologists in cognitive processes.

Therefore we contend that study of the *Project* throws light on many hypotheses fundamental to later formulations and allows review and revision in the light of current neuropsychological knowledge.

In short, we believe that psychoanalysts will profit by sympathetic study of Freud's neuropsychology in the *Project* which is in important respects considerably more explicit than Chapter 7 of *The Interpretation of Dreams* (1900), their current source for metapsychological understanding. And we also urge all psychologists interested in cognitive processes to review the *Project* for currently relevant, comprehensive and detailed theories of thinking and consciousness.

How did we come to view Freud's *Project* as a document of value for our time and not just an historical oddity of closely packed interlacing ideas jotted down with urgency and then forgotten? Two ideas help immeasurably. The first, baldly stated, is the growing dissatisfaction in the psychoanalytic literature with metapsychological theory. This dissatisfaction led, as already mentioned, to a realization that the theory had now become a tangle of clinically oriented 'psychological' conceptions larded with 'metapsychological' mechanisms. Once the distinction had been attained it became obvious that metapsychological conceptions were in fact neuropsychological in origin, that they remained biological in spirit if not always in word 'to the very end' and thus open to constructive criticism and change.

The second idea is neurological and deals with the concept of cathexis. This idea (Pribram, 1962) states simply that cathexis is to be identified with local charges of neural energy, graded electrotonic excitations of nerve tissue, about which today's neurophysiology has a great deal to say (Pribram, 1971). This identity is adduced from the fact that Freud, in the *Project*, consistently opposes cathexis which 'fills' the neuron to the conducted nerve impulse which 'empties', discharges it. What follows is that the metapsychology, the psychoanalytic models of mechanism are therefore sophisticated neuropsychological models as well. From this the suggestion arises that some of the more basic psychoanalytic propositions such as the place of drive, affect and wish in motivational structure could conceivably derive strength from conceptualizations and tests made at the neurological level of investigation (see for instance Holt, 1967; Klein, 1967; Pribram, 1965). Should this prove to be feasible, the accusation some biological scientists level at psychoanalysis – that a non-scientific closed-shop attitude pervades – would be met as far as the psychoanalytic metapsychology is concerned and on the biologist's home grounds at that: the connections to biology of a large segment of psychoanalytic theory – the metapsychological concepts – will be seen as less vague and therefore less monolithic, capable of clarification in many specific and particular instances – as e.g. in the proposed mechanisms of unpleasure, of affect and of attention – through observation and experiment. The *Project* appears to us as the key point of departure for accomplishing this.

We decided, therefore, to make a thorough exposition of the *Project* but not just as a 'book review'. First, we organized Freud's concepts according to advances in scientific thought that have occurred since 1895, advances such as information measurement, and control theory. Second, we adduced current behavioural and neurophysiological data to support or to contradict those concepts. We believe that this manner of presentation makes the *Project* currently useful and truly a 'Preface to Contemporary Cognitive Theory and Neuropsychology'.

By way of introduction, some of the currents of the scientific *Zeitgeist* within which Freud worked, by now clarified by a number of authors (see Amacher, 1965), need to be re-stated. Freud was a member of the physicalist group of Viennese neurologists who looked to Helmholtz and to Mach for guidance. Their aim was to describe, as far as possible, biological phenomena in the terms used in the physical, i.e. the natural, sciences. This aim received support from the fact that *neural* activity could be studied by electrically stimulating and recording from biological tissue and that the effects of such stimulations on chemical processes in the organism's body could be determined.

But Freud was not concerned only with biology – his patients had psychological difficulties. Work with Meynert, Brentano (Bernfeld, 1949; Merlan, 1945, 1949) and Charcot made it clear that behaviour is motivated – intentional – and that psychological processes such as thinking *could* be systematically investigated by the application of appropriate techniques – e.g. by hypnosis and by observations of the seemingly unrelated associations that occur during problem solving behaviour. Freud's tutelage in neuropsychiatry by Meynert, his tenure in Charcot's clinic and the influence this experience had on his career is well documented (Jones, 1957) but

The traces of Brentano's *Act Psychology* are less obvious and have never been explicitly discussed. Yet, the central position of instinctual drives in Freud's theory parallels Brentano's interpretation (which contrasts sharply with that of Anglo-Saxon empiricists) of both stimulation and response in terms of acts of intending. In the early phases of Freud's *ego psychology*, Brentano's influence seems even more striking. The term intention crops up, the problem of reality testing leads to an analysis of the 'belief in reality' (Freud, 1916b, p. 146) along Brentano-like lines, and the distinctions between what is perceived and what is conceived, what is real and what is only thought, etc., come into play. This influence pervades the *Papers on Metapsychology* (1911b, 1912, 1914b, 1915a, 1915b, 1915c, 1916a, 1917a). And although Freud deliberately refused to have anything to do with philosophy, he did acquire some familiarity with it through Brentano. In one of the few specific references he makes to philosophy he characterizes psychoanalysis (and particularly its concept of unconscious determination) as the psychological counterpart of Kant's philosophical views (Freud, 1915c, p. 104). Indeed, the epistemological implications of psychoanalysis are closest to Kant (see Rapaport, 1947) and most remote from Anglo-Saxon empiricism.

(Rapaport, 1960, p. 13)

Freud's neurological experience made it clear that the *brain* was the prime instrument of the organization of psychological function. Behaviourism had not come to psychology: the distinctions between verbal reports of introspections and directly observable behaviour had yet to be clearly enunciated. None the less, Freud clearly distinguished between the conscious and unconscious determinants of behaviour: he maintained that conscious and unconscious processes could be distinguished in terms of different organizations within the central nervous system.

In making his model Freud thus became involved with an issue that continues to confront neurological and behavioural science as well as philosophy – the mind-body problem. Freud wanted above all to maintain his self-image as a scientist, a self-image derived in good part from Helmholtz's biological physicalism and Brentano's observational psychology. Rather than side-step the issue, he faced it directly in the *Project*. Only later did the neurological points become largely implicit in the metapsychological propositions.

Consciousness is the conception central to the mind-brain issue – an issue dealt with in considerable detail in the *Project*: conscious awareness results when the rules of attention operate. Freud's position on the relationship between consciousness, behaviour and brain is made clear. He wrote:

A word on the relation of this theory of consciousness to others. According to an advanced mechanistic theory, consciousness is a mere appendage to physiologico-psychical processes, and its omission would make no alteration

in the psychical passage [of events]. According to another theory, consciousness is the subjective side of all psychical events and is thus inseparable from
the physiological mental processes. The theory developed here lies between
these two. Here consciousness is the subjective side of one *part* [emphasis ours]
of the physical processes in the nervous system, namely of the ω [*perceptual*]
processes; and the omission of consciousness does not leave psychical events
unaltered but involves the omission of the contribution from ω.

(S.E., p. 311)[1]

Again,

On this view the perceptual processes would *eo ipso* [from their very nature]
involve consciousness and would only produce their further psych[*ological*]
effects *after* becoming conscious.

(S.E., p. 389)

Consciousness is crucial in relating the physical and the mental
universe of discourse. Freud felt that in the *Project* he could handle a
great number of attributes of the psychological process through a
physicalist, quantitative approach – the unit of quantity referring to
an amount of neural excitation. Consciousness, however, did not easily
lend itself to this quantitative approach:

. . . every psychological theory, apart from what it achieves from the point
of view of natural science, must fulfil yet another major requirement. It
should explain to us what we are aware of, in the most puzzling fashion,
through our 'consciousness'; and, since this consciousness knows nothing of
what we have so far been assuming – quantities and neurones – it should
explain this lack of knowledge to us as well.

(S.E., pp. 307–8)

As we shall see in Chapters 1 and 3, Freud solved this dilemma by
suggesting that, when synaptic resistance has become minimal, nerve
tissue is sensitive to periodicities, i.e. patterns of excitation, and that it is
these which are the neural substrate of consciousness. He calls such
patterns 'quality'. The total process leading to awareness is yet more
complicated. Only through the operation of two feedback loops
initiated by the biological rules of attention (see Ch. 3) do patterns of
excitation become sufficiently emphasized to allow this process to

---

[1]Unless otherwise noted, all quotations from Freud's works are taken from Volume 1
of the *Standard Edition of the Complete Psychological Works of Sigmund Freud*, edited and
translated by James Strachey, Hogarth Press, twenty-four volumes. All passages that
appear in brackets are insertions by either Strachey or ourselves. When by ourselves
the passages are italicized. When we have emphasized a passage of Freud's by using
italics, this is so stated in the passage.

come to fruition. The problem as a whole is faced in the *Project* in a highly specific and detailed fashion:

If we keep firmly to the fact that our consciousness furnishes only *qualities*, whereas [*physical*] science recognizes only *quantities*, a characterization of the ω [*perceptual*] neurones emerges, as though by rule of three [*rule of hierarchy might be a better translation*]. For whereas [*physical*] science has set about the task of tracing all the *qualities* of our sensations back to *external quantities*, it is to be expected from the structure of the nervous system that it consists of contrivances for transforming external *quantity* into quality. . . .

(S.E., p. 309)

What is so novel about Freud's handling of the problem of consciousness? Certainly not the attribution of awareness to the functioning of a part of the central nervous apparatus. The *Zeitgeist* obtaining in Vienna during the 1890s is displayed in great detail in Exner's *Entwurf* (1894) – that other *Project* which provided such an 'important immediate stimulus' (Jones, 1957, p. 380) to Freud's own gigantic undertaking. Cortex is certainly repeatedly referred to by Exner as the organ of consciousness; diagrams of the operation of the process are everywhere (e.g. p. 193).

What then is unique in the *Project*? Freud's twist lies in his unveiling of the importance, the meaningfulness of *unconsciously determined behaviour* as an indicator of a scientifically accessible *process*, whereas others had merely concerned themselves with the obvious, i.e. the conscious. What is unique is the fact that he turned the whole argument around:

We at once become clear about a postulate which has been guiding us up to now. We have been treating psychical processes as something that could dispense with . . . awareness through consciousness, as something that exists independently of such awareness. We are prepared to find that some of our assumptions are not confirmed through consciousness. If we do not let ourselves be confused on that account, it follows, from the postulate of consciousness providing neither complete nor trustworthy knowledge of the neuronal processes, that these are in the first instance to be regarded to their whole extent as unconscious and are to be inferred like other natural things.

(S.E., p. 308)

This solution to the mind-brain-behaviour problem is not very different from the superventionist (or interventionist) emergent property theory proposed recently by Sperry (1969). The current theory is based

20

on observations and experiments with patients who had their corpus callosum sectioned, producing not only a 'split brain' but two separable states. Eccles (1970) has interpreted these data to suggest that only the state regulated with the left, language producing, hemisphere should be termed 'conscious' and that the non-linguistic hemisphere is responsible for unconscious processes, while Sperry emphasizes, on the basis of non-linguistic behavioural indicators, the separate 'consciousness' of each.

Furthermore, a series of studies by Weiskrantz and Warrington (1974) has shown that patients with hemianopia due to restricted lesions of the occipital cortex can make remarkably good instrumental discriminative responses to objects displayed in the blind part of their visual field. Not only brightness but place and contour can be discriminated. Yet when these patients are asked what they see they reply 'nothing at all'. They say they are responding on some vague non-verbalizable 'feel' and that they are not 'conscious' of any visual excitation in their blind hemifield. These recent developments suggest we look seriously once again at the detailed proposals as to the neural mechanisms involved in consciousness put forward in the *Project* (see Chs. 2 and 3) – especially as the current speculations by Sperry and Eccles are so totally devoid of such proposals.

Enough has been said by way of introduction to indicate what it is we want to accomplish in this monograph. A formal presentation of our purpose reads: Freud's *Psychology for Neurologists*, his *Entwurf einer Psychologie*, the *Project*, is an important document. The hypotheses derived from this purpose can be phrased as follows: many terms used throughout that part of psychoanalytic theory which deals with mechanism are given operational definitions in the *Project*. As these usually involve neurological as well as behavioural referents, the document is, in a sense, a Rosetta stone for those interested in making communication between these realms of discourse possible. In addition, the *Project* contains early conceptions of processes which in many instances anticipate by years the later formulations made not only by Freud but by other psychologists and neuroscientists; in some cases these are more explicit and detailed explications of mechanism than can be found in any other of Freud's writings or that have been attained by others. Thus any psychological theory influenced by psychoanalytic concepts of mechanism, the metapsychology, would not have taken its present form without the formulations set forth in the *Project*. Cognitive theory can thus profit from study of the formulations set forth in the *Project*, and the crux of these formulations is that they are based on neurological as well as on behavioural evidence. In fact, this neurological base of the mechanisms invoked in psychoanalytic theory proposed in 1895, which remain essentially unchanged though obscured throughout Freud's later writings, furnishes innumerable opportunities for tests of the validity of current conceptions such as 'drive reduction', 'ego strength' and 'wish fulfilment' and the attentional mechanism of 'reality testing'.

Finally, our purpose is to organize in a current theoretical frame concepts initiated in the *Project* and thus provide a *Preface to Contemporary Cognitive Theory and Neuropsychology.*

[1]

THE REGULATORY
PRINCIPLES AND
CONTROL THEORY

SOME CONCEPTUAL DISTINCTIONS

The *Project* is based on two basic postulates: the first is the concept of inertia; the second, the neuron doctrine. The concept of inertia becomes developed into a host of regulatory principles; the neuron doctrine provides the mechanisms of the metapsychology. We are, as was Freud, therefore faced with the task of making whole cloth of woof and warp. Our choice is to let the regulatory principles guide the organization of the manuscript while neuropsychology makes up its content.

Regulation is synonymous with control and there have been significant advances in control theory, often called cybernetics, since World War II. Many of these advances are highly technical and therefore unfamiliar to a general audience. We need here to touch upon those developments relevant to understanding psychoanalytic metapsychology and hope the reader will bear with us if we have not always succeeded in making a difficult topic crystal clear. The most generally known innovation in control theory has been the formal description of the concept of feedback (e.g. see Miller, Galanter and Pribram, 1960), a circular process initiated by a test, a matching of two settings. When there is mismatch, one of the settings becomes fixed while the other triggers an operation which continues until a match is produced. Thus a test-operate-test-exit sequence, a TOTE, characterizes the feedback: for example, if the setting of a thermostat and that of room temperature are incongruent, i.e. mismatch, a furnace is either turned on or off until congruence is established.

More recently, another, equally useful conception, feedforward (e.g. see MacKay, 1969; Mittelstaedt, 1968; and Pribram, 1971) has been found important. In feedforward control, an operation proceeds to a

23

predetermined end point. For example, in most apartments, the furnace continues to operate for fixed periods, irrespective of local temperature conditions. (See also Fig. 1.)

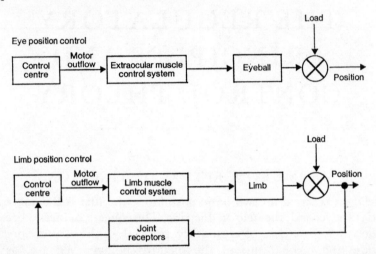

Fig. 1. Outline of eyeball and limb position control systems. Eye position is an example of an open-loop feedforward mechanism. Limb position is an example of a feedback mechanism.

The distinction between feedback and feedforward has been extremely useful in analysing engineering and biological systems which ordinarily are composed of complex combinations of feedback and feedforward processes. Two types of combinations have been extensively studied. In one, feedback processes become associated, multiply linked, with each other producing an extremely stable system resistant to change (i.e. they exhibit inertia). An engineering example of such a system is the multilinking of power plants in the north-eastern United States which guards against frequent local disruptions, though it is vulnerable to occasional massive failure. Biologically, physiological drive systems have been found to display this type of organization. Thus food intake, muscular activity, temperature regulation and water metabolism are interdependent regulatory mechanisms which, as a rule, operate to maintain basal temperature constant. The associative links that make up this and similar systems have been studied extensively (e.g. see review by Brobeck, 1963) and their operating characteristics thoroughly analysed (Ashby, 1960). We shall see that the *Project* anticipates these efforts by distinguishing clearly those processes

24

based on associative structure from others of a more complex nature.

Complex combinations based primarily on feedforward processes are ubiquitous; they constitute our computer technology. For the most part, such combinations contain feedbacks as well. Biologically, combinations of feedforwards occur in parallel, processing signals simultaneously by virtue of overlapping neighbourhood interactions, and constitute one class of cognitive processes (see Neisser, 1967; Eccles, 1967; Pribram, 1971). When feedback loops are included, hierarchical sequential arrangements called Plans or programmes are constituted (Miller, Galanter and Pribram, 1960). Parallel and hierarchical processing mechanisms provide the foundations of contemporary cognitive theory and, as we shall see, are spelled out in surprising detail in the *Project*.

But the feedback-feedforward distinction is not the only one relevant to the *Project* that is made in control theory. Perhaps even more seminal has been the distinction between energy and information. The distinction is, as we hope to demonstrate, crucial to any understanding of psychological mechanisms. It originally derived from thermodynamics, where the first law deals with the conservation of energy and the second with its organization. The first law reads that every interaction among systems is constrained by the fact that any action begets an equal and opposite reaction. It is a law describing inertia, a concept which becomes the first postulate of the *Project*. The second law deals with the amount of change produced in the organization of the energy systems involved in these interactions. Thus, when heat is produced as a result of friction in the interaction between a vehicle and a roadbed, there is loss of organization since the molecular structure of heat is more random than that of either vehicle or road. This dissipation of organization is measured as entropy.

A similar distinction became useful in communication engineering when it was found that the amount of energy expended in powering a system had no direct relationship to the amount of communication – i.e. information processing taking place. A radio consumes essentially as much energy in emitting static as it does in communicating a symphony; a television set does not increase its consumption when a sports event replaces the test pattern. The amount of organization that characterizes a communication was given a measure called 'information' by Claude Shannon and Warren Weaver (1949). Information measurement allowed the specification of the fidelity with which a system transmits a communication.

Because of the success of information measurement in communication

25

systems there have been periodic attempts to re-evaluate the psycho-analytic metapsychology (viewed as an intrapsychic communications network) in 'information processing' terms. As will be made clear in the immediately following pages, we feel that despite the merit of these attempts, there is also considerable danger that energy concepts such as mental work and effort basic to the development of any coherent cognitive theory (see e.g. McFarland, 1971; Kahneman, 1973; Pribram and McGuinness, 1975) be prematurely ruled out before they are given adequate trial. In biology, as noted above, homeostatic processes, oscillating phenomena such as biological rhythms and clocks, load adjusting mechanisms such as those regulating muscular contraction, have all been shown dependent on feedback organization (Pribram, 1971).

Recall that the essential characteristic of such systems is that they depend upon a match between two settings. A mismatch produces an error signal which controls the operation of the system until equilibrium, match, is re-established. This homeostatic conservation of equilibrium is akin to that described by the first law of thermodynamics which states that the conservation of *energy* is maintained by an 'equal and opposite reaction'. (Information concepts, by contrast, have often been linked to the second law, and in fact, information has been termed by Brillouin (1962) neg-entropy. See also von Foerster, 1965.) Energy concepts are therefore appropriate to description and understanding of feedback organizations, and in fact are regularly used as, for example, in describing the 'effort' or 'work' involved in load adjusting mechanisms.

Confusion has arisen because there has been a tendency to label 'error', the mismatch signal, 'information'. But 'error' has nothing in common with Shannon–Weaver 'information': the amount of information contained in a message does not depend on processing its errors. Ashby (1963, pp. 127 ff.) details the distinction in terms of the constraints (limits on the independence of the functioning parts) operating on the processing system, constraints on variety. Information is a measure of variety; redundancy (repetition), a measure of the constraints. Information thus refers to the content of a communication while redundancy reflects the context or code in which information is communicated. Feedback organizations constrain systems to equilibrium. Thus error becomes a term denoting redundancy or lack thereof, not information. When a long-distance conversation is interrupted by a periodic whoosh, the constraint, the context in which the information is relayed becomes disturbed, the conversation becomes unintelligible and a mismatch is conveyed to the sender who then repeats the same information more slowly with greater emphasis and perhaps several times, changing the structure of the constraints operating during the conversation without altering its content, the amount of information.

In short, feedback mechanisms are error-processing organizations constrained to equilibrium and thus energy concepts such as 'load', 'power', 'work', 'effort', 'degrees of freedom' and 'dependence' or 'association' as measures of constraint, are applicable. Feedback mechanisms can become associated, multilinked enhancing the constraints or they can operate in parallel as part of feedforward organizations that reduce constraint (Ashby, 1960; Pribram, 1971, Ch. 5).

By contrast, feedforward organizations are programmes that, once started, ordinarily run themselves to completion unless interrupted or scrapped. Whenever a communication system becomes sufficiently complex, a 'switchboard' is required to channel the communication appropriately among senders and receivers. This switchboard or central processor was found to be readily adapted to another capability, that of computing relationships among communications. Initially this meant simply adding one communication to another but this operation was easily transmuted into subtraction, multiplication and division. Further development led to spatial, two dimensional adding, i.e., superimposition and correlation, as for instance with IBM punch cards which are overlayed (added) and a signal is generated only when the holes in all of the cards match. Finally, by virtue of the installation of a memory mechanism, the capability to list (a sequential communication that can be 'punched' on tape instead of a card) and cross reference among lists gave rise to modern programming possibilities. These were further enhanced in time sharing systems by the imposition of executive programmes that are superordinate to others and determine the order in which a set of programmes is to run through the system.

The conceptions brought forth in the *Project* are surprisingly easy to organize according to whether they are primarily feedback or feedforward mechanisms; and whether the feedforward processes are straightforward or whether they are controlled by an executive. The reason may well be historical: much of modern control theory derived its initial impetus from Norbert Wiener (1948) who trained in the neurophysiological laboratories of Walter Cannon (1927, 1929) on problems of homeostasis – Cannon's name for the 'inertia' shown by the organism's internal environment.

We thus find in the *Project* that regulations involving the internal environment can be discussed (see this chapter) as error sensitive

27

feedback processes, but that regulatory controls involving memory mechanisms are more readily discussed (see Ch. 2) in terms of programmed, feedforward, information processes, which become regulated by an executive. Perhaps more unexpected is the description in the *Project* (see Ch. 3) of the feedback mechanisms that control conscious awareness through selective attention which rival those proposed by recent cognitive theorists (e.g. Bruner, 1957; Sokolov, 1960; Miller, Galanter and Pribram, 1960; Neisser, 1967; Pribram, 1971) both in overall conception and detail of the mechanism described.

We therefore propose to cast one of the most important and basic distinctions in the psychoanalytic metapsychology – the separation between primary and secondary processes – partly in terms of the load adjusting or error processing vs programming or information processing distinction. We introduce the topic shortly and develop it fully in the remainder of this monograph. Usually, as in physical systems, biological controls are exercised by a combination of feedforward and feedback. None the less, the distinction reflects to an extraordinary degree conceptualizations to be found in the *Project*. Thus in this chapter we take up the organization of primary processes such as drive, pain, unpleasure, and the initial production of affect and wish, as based on error processing, feedback mechanisms. Chapter 2 deals with the development of secondary process behaviour, from wishes, which are simple memory-motive structures, through the operation of defences and satisfactions, to behaviour controlled by an executive ego. Chapter 3 begins our concern with a mix of primary and secondary processes: it returns us to error processing and feedback, in the genesis of consciousness through the operation of primary attention and judgement, precursors to perception, and then develops these into the secondary process of reality testing and the willed, intentional execution of specific actions. In Chapter 4 we take up the theory of thinking essentially in terms of programmed – i.e. secondary – processes with primary process components, leaving to Chapter 5 the more difficult concepts that relate primary associative and dissociative mechanisms to 'energy' concepts *per se* such as error, load and effort. Here also, however, we end with 'compromise' formations, special mixes of primary and secondary processes found in psychopathology.

Within this framework, we now turn to an examination in some detail of the regulatory principles as they are conceived in the *Project*.

THE FIRST POSTULATE

Freud begins the construction of his model much as did Sherrington (1947) with a discussion of the organization of reflex automatic behaviour. However, where Sherrington compares the properties of neurons with experimentally derived properties of the behaviour of the spinal animal, Freud compares the characteristics of neurons with the results of clinical observations of patients 'especially where excessively intense ideas are concerned – in hysteria and obsessions, in which, as we shall see, the quantitative characteristic emerges more plainly than in the normal' (p. 295). He goes on to develop a model to account for the clinical phenomena in terms of 'the conception of neuronal excitation as quantity in a state of flow' (p. 296). Further,

> . . . the nervous system, as inheritor of the general irritability of protoplasm, . . . makes use of this $Q\dot{\eta}$ [*quantity of excitation in neurons*] which it has . . . acquired, by giving it off through a connecting path to the muscular mechanisms, and in that way keeps itself free from stimulus. . . .

> This is the principle of neuronal inertia: that neurones tend to divest themselves of Q. . . . The principle of inertia is, however, [*breached* (translated as *broken through*)] . . . owing to another circumstance. With an [increasing] complexity of the interior [of the organism], the nervous system receives stimuli from the somatic element itself – endogenous stimuli – which have equally to be discharged. These have their origin in the cells of the body and give rise to the major needs: hunger, respiration, sexuality. From these the organism cannot withdraw as it does from external stimuli; it cannot employ their Q for flight from the stimulus. They only cease subject to particular conditions, which must be realized in the external world. (Cf., for instance, the need for nourishment.) In order to accomplish such an action (which deserves to be named 'specific'), an effort is required which is independent of endogenous $Q\dot{\eta}$ and in general greater, since the individual is being subjected to conditions which may be described as *the exigencies of life*. In consequence, the nervous system is obliged to abandon its original trend to inertia (that is, to bringing the level [of $Q\dot{\eta}$] to zero). It must put up with [maintaining] a store of $Q\dot{\eta}$ sufficient to meet the demand for a specific action. Nevertheless, the manner in which it does this shows that the same trend persists, modified into an endeavour at least to keep the $Q\dot{\eta}$ as low as possible and to guard against any increase of it – that is, to keep it constant. All the functions of the nervous system can be comprised either under the aspect of the primary function or of the secondary one imposed by the exigencies of life.

(S.E., pp. 296–7)

29

Freud thus began to derive a set of regulatory principles for behavioural processes as well as a model of brain function (see Ch. 2) from his comparisons between what was then known about neurophysiology and behavioural observations. In this respect also his procedure is similar to Sherrington's. Sherrington derived such principles as the antagonism and the coordination among reflexes, sensory fusion and the like and such models as synapse and receptive field. Freud's regulatory principles invoked concepts such as quantity of neural excitation and discharge, specific action, storage and effort – in short, the primary and secondary functions of the nervous system which were to become developed into the concepts of primary and secondary processes (see below). His models invoked a central nervous system memory-motive structure based on synaptic facilitations and resistances, a neurochemical mechanism of drive and unpleasure, and a brain wave mechanism of perception. As we hope to show, these concepts and models are as viable today in initiating inquiry into complex psychological processes as Sherrington's have been in leading to an exploration of sensory-motor function.

The basic tenets of Freud's regulatory principles – crucially based upon his economic point of view – have recently been severely challenged. Holt (1967), Klein (1967), and Peterfreund and Schwartz (1971) have, each in his own way, proposed that the earlier regulatory principles be scrapped for a more modern approach based on other parts of Freud's theory (such as wish fulfilment). All criticisms take issue with the concept 'quantity of energy' (but see also Colby, 1955) as being antiquated and thus preclude regulatory principles based on an energy concept *per se*. For many years we shared this view and for this reason, among others, put our manuscript on the *Project* aside for a decade: for, if in fact Freud's first postulate is so far in error, what is left of this theory?

During this decade we have come to a somewhat more positive view – the view set out in the introduction: it is true that the theory initially presented in the *Project* has become distorted over the years, yet delving into its origins can provide the basis for a sophisticated cognitive theory. Specifically, with regard to the energy concept, because the metapsychology became increasingly divorced from its neurophysiological roots, 'psychical energy' became the progenitor of 'psychical' concepts intertwining the psychological and metapsychological theories of psychoanalysis. The energy concept belongs solely to the metapsychology. It must therefore be examined from the view of contemporary neurophysiology.

THE ENERGY CONCEPT

Let us look first at the criticisms already available, criticisms which to us now look superficial:

Current psychoanalytic theory essentially represents a hydrodynamic model. Uniting the anthropomorphic entities in the mind are psychic energies with fluid properties and with anthropomorphic qualitative characteristics, e.g., sexual and aggressive qualitative characteristics. These qualitative characteristics or identities can be transferred or transformed.

Because of its basically anthropocentric position, its hydrodynamic character, its primitive anthropomorphism, and its fundamental conceptual divorce from biology and from all of evolutionary time, current psychoanalytic theory is a very limited theory. It cannot develop an adequate learning theory nor an adequate theory of the psychoanalytic process, and it cannot be meaningfully linked to modern neurophysiology.

(Peterfreund and Schwartz, 1971, p. 85)

We agree with the diagnosis that the part of current psychoanalytic theory dealing with mechanisms, viewed by Peterfreund and Schwartz as a unitary hydrodynamic anthropomorphic melange, is badly in need of revision. Further, this also applies to clinical theory, to the extent that it has become contaminated with such poorly defined mechanisms. But we would urge that contemporary psychoanalytic theory has come to its sorry state by ignoring its roots. Freud is, of course, particularly responsible: he never published the *Project* and in his subsequent writings he seriously attempted to expunge the biological and neurophysiological formulations that gave rise to his metapsychology. But since 1950 the German edition of the *Project* has been available and since 1954 the Basic Books edition of *The Origins of Psycho-Analysis*, which includes an English version of the *Project* as an appendix, has been circulated. In 1962 and also in 1965 Pribram again called the attention of the scientific community to the *Project* and how through it psychoanalytic theory could be related to 'learning theory' and 'modern neurophysiology' – yet Peterfreund and Schwartz, for example, despite their serious concern, published an otherwise provocative and comprehensive monograph in 1971 *completely* ignoring the *Project*!

Compare the quotation from Peterfreund and Schwartz which accurately reflects the vague view of the energy concept as it is held in psychoanalysis, psychiatry and clinical psychology today (and by the community of the [en]counter culture, as well) with the detailed definition of $Q\dot{\eta}$, quantity of energy, provided in the *Project* and quoted

at the beginning of this section (p. 29). Strachey felt that understanding the nature of Q to be so important that, for his most recent
translation of the *Project* (1966), he developed an appendix (Appendix
C, S.E., vol. 1, p. 392) devoted to the problem. In this scholarly
analysis Strachey points out that one might be easily misled into
believing that

> ... Q was simply electricity and that the two ways of measuring it corres-
> ponded to amperage and voltage. It is true that some eighteen months before
> the composition of the *Project*, in his first paper on the neuro-psychoses of
> defence (1894), he had made a vague comparison between something that
> was a precursor of Q and 'an electric charge spread over the surface of a
> body' (*Standard Ed.*, *3*, 60). It is also true that Breuer, in his theoretical
> contribution to *Studies on Hysteria* (1895) (published only a few months before
> the *Project* was written) had devoted some space to an electrical analogy to
> the 'excitations' in the 'conductive paths of the brain' (ibid., *2*, 193-4).
> Nevertheless, nowhere in the *Project* is there a word to suggest that any such
> idea was present in Freud's mind. On the contrary, he repeatedly emphasizes
> the fact that the nature of 'neuronal motion' is unknown to us. (See, for
> instance, pp. 372, 379, and 387.)
>
> (S.E., p. 393)

Is Strachey's conclusion justified? Only partly, we believe. Freud
was a neurologist with extensive laboratory experience. Neuroelectric
measurements of electrotonic potentials and propagated nerve impulses
were not only commonplace in 1895 but also of sufficient recency to
capture the imagination of the neuroscientists of that time. Thus
Pflüger, one of Freud's sponsors, published a monograph on electrotonic
potentials in 1859. Why then did Freud not clearly identify a quantity of
neural excitation with its electrical manifestations? For just the same
reason that we, today, write 'with its electrical manifestation'. The
basic property of 'neuronal motion' (energy in motion was a term
popular with the physicalists) is neurochemical and in 1895 the
neurochemistry of hyperpolarization and depolarization and the
membrane characteristics that give rise to a propagated nerve impulse
were in their infancy. Thus the neurochemical nature of Q could not
be described, only its manifestation in electrical activity. A few passages
from Schäfer's *Textbook of Physiology* published in 1898-1900 concisely
present the state of knowledge of that period:

> *Phenomena of the excitatory state.* The excitatory state evoked by a stimulus
> manifests itself in nerve fibre by electromotive changes, and, as far as our
> present knowledge goes, by these only. This state may spread to successive

portions of the nerve beyond the region subjected to the action of the stimulus, the spread being accompanied by similar electromotive changes. All theories as to the nature of the hidden events which take place in the living tissue, and constitute this excitatory state, must embrace these demonstrable facts.

The conception of such an excitable living tissue as nerve, implies that of a molecular state which is in stable equilibrium; this equilibrium can be readily upset by an external agency, the stimulus, but the term 'stable' expresses the fact that a change in any direction must be succeeded by one of opposite character, this being the return of the living structure to its previous state. Thus the electrical manifestation of the excitatory state is one whose duration depends upon the time during which the external agent is able to upset and retain in a new poise the living equilibrium, and if this is extremely brief, then the recoil of the tissue causes such manifestation to be itself of very short duration. Whether our conception of the actual physico-chemical conditions of this living equilibrium, whose disturbance is excitation, be mechanical (du Bois-Reymond, Pflueger), chemical (Hering, Biedermann), electrochemical (Bernstein, Hermann, Boruttau), the above statement is equally true. No departure from the normal in consequence of excitation takes place without being succeeded by the opposite condition.

> (Francis Gotch in *Schäfer*,
> 1900, vol. 2, p. 453)

Compare these (and other) paragraphs from Schäfer's text with similar statements in the *Project* already quoted and regarding the manifestation of Q in the nervous system to the following:

The principle of inertia [p. 296] finds its expression in the hypothesis of a *current* passing from the cell's paths of conduction or processes [dendrites] to the axis-cylinder. A single neurone is thus a model of the whole nervous system with its dichotomy of structure, the axis-cylinder being the organ of discharge. The secondary function [of the nervous system], however, which calls for the accumulation of $Q\dot{\eta}$ [p. 297], is made possible by the assumption of *resistances* [*emphasis ours*] which oppose discharge; and the structure of neurones makes it probable that the resistances are to be located in the *contacts* [between one neurone and another], which in this way assume the value of *barriers*.

> (S.E., p. 298)

Can anyone really maintain in the face of these quotations that Freud the neuroscientist was developing a hydrodynamic model? Can anyone really doubt that Freud was referring to ordinary, garden variety neurophysiology? Can anyone really hold, as Strachey insists, that 'Nevertheless, nowhere in the *Project* is there a word to suggest that any such idea was present in Freud's mind'?

We will proceed here on the assumption that Freud did mean what he seems to mean – that *current* means not a current of fluid but action currents of electrical nerve impulses (which were at that time measured by means of galvanometers – instruments used to determine amperage, a measure of electrical current); that when he speaks of '*Niveau*' (which Strachey cautiously translates as 'level' and calls it a mistranslation to call it potential – footnote 1, p. 393) Freud means level of *potential*; that when he speaks of *resistance* he means resistance to the passage of a nerve impulse. In short we subscribe to the idea that Freud the physicalist was in fact attempting an Ohm's Law of neural function but since the quantitative data to do so were not available he refrained from actually writing the equation.

In summary, quantity, Q, we believe refers to physical and chemical quantity of energy (see e.g. quotations under drive, p. 44), that $Q\dot{\eta}$ is its neuroelectric manifestation which can accrue as a *potential* within a neuron, become action currents of nerve impulses, which when they overcome the *resistances* at contacts between neurons, discharge the neuron. Contemporary neurophysiology could find little to fault in this outline of nervous system function. Thus the *Project* contains exactly what the critics of the current melange of psychoanalytic dogma are seeking (e.g. Colby, 1955; Peterfreund and Schwartz, 1971): a biological (physical) definition of the energy concept which can be 'meaningfully linked to modern neurophysiology'.

However, this root definition of the energy concept by no means solves all of the problems associated with contemporary interpretations and uses of the conception of that vague and mystical '*psychic energy*'. Only recently have distinctions been attained which allow a clear understanding of what is involved. Freud, of course, had no access to these recent conceptual discoveries; furthermore, neither have his critics fully digested them.

As noted earlier, the essential distinction that must be made is between error and information processing mechanisms. The question can thus be put as to when it is appropriate to use error processsing concepts such as energy, effort, etc., and when to use information concepts. One might think, in view of the contemporary confusion, that the *Project* would have nothing to say that would clarify the issue. But this is not so.

So far I have regarded it only as the transference of $Q\dot{\eta}$ from one neurone to another. But it must have still another characteristic, of a temporal nature; for the mechanics of the physicists have allowed this temporal characteristic to the other motions of masses in the external world as well. I speak of this as *period* for short. . . .

Where do these differences of *period* spring from? Everything points to the sense-organs, whose *qualities [emphasis ours]* seem to be represented precisely by different periods of neuronal motion. The sense-organs act not only as Q-screens, like all nerve-ending apparatuses, but also as *sieves*; for they allow the stimulus through from only certain processes with a particular period.

(S.E., p. 310)

Today we would talk of the wave length of sensory (e.g. visual or auditory) stimulus; we would talk of coding the *information* transduced by the sense organ in a pulse code or a frequency code (see e.g. Perkel and Bullock, 1968) of nerve impulses for transmission and so on. But the basic idea is the same whether we characterize the pattern as a period (or its reciprocal, frequency) or in terms of information. What is, of course, added by information measurement is precision, a way of measuring amount, clarity in conception and application to a wide variety of systems. These developments should enhance metapsychological theory, however, not disrupt it because the fundamental distinction was built in from the beginning.

As already noted (p. 27), information concepts are most appropriately applicable to mechanisms dealing with cognitive, secondary processes. Information concepts are less applicable to the issues developed around primary associative processes involving the multi-linking of feedback loops. Here, energy, Q, becomes directly relevant and is quantitatively defined in control theory as the capacity for work necessary to change a system constrained to remain in its current state. Work is a measure of the rate of changing such a system.

Of course, Freud is not alone in invoking energy concepts in psychology. McFarland (1971), in a book that relates control theory to behaviour theory, reviews (pp. 215 and 220–22) succinctly the various formulations of the energy concept (e.g. McDougall, 1923; Lorenz, 1937, 1950; Tinbergen, 1951; as well as Freud, 1933, 1940) and the criticisms that have been levied against them. None the less he argues that 'a rigorous definition of motivational states makes an energy concept logically inevitable' (p. 215) in behaviour theory provided the concept is kept strictly (i.e. logically and mathematically) analogous to its use in the physical sciences.

McFarland goes on to give rigorous methods for utilizing such analyses in terms of optimization principles, the functional rather than the causal role of energy in such formulations (i.e. energy is inferred as resulting from rather than leading to observed changes in systems) and examples of actual procedures from his experiments. Pribram has recently applied such an analysis to derive the concept of effort in cognitive processing from his own and other's experiments dealing with attention (Pribram and McGuinness, 1975).

Further, McFarland points out (p. 197) that von Holst and Mittelstaedt's (1950) reafference theory based on experiments analysing the optomotor reflex of a fly is essentially a view similar (though more precise) to that of Helmholtz's (1867) 'outflow' open loop, feedforward theory (Fig. 2).

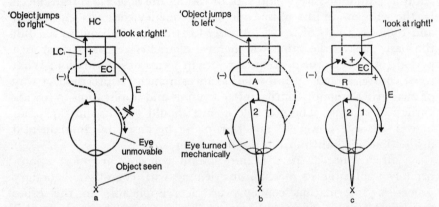

Fig. 2. Illustration of von Holst's experiments with the human eye. HC = higher centre, LC = lower centre, EC = efference copy, E = efferent message, A = afferent message, R = reafferent message. (a) Illustrates the situation when the eye is narcotized, (b) the situation when the eye is moved mechanically, (c) represents situations (a) and (b) combined in such a way that the two effects cancel each other. (From von Holst, 1954)

We have already noted that Freud was attempting to build a 'psychology' modelled in the Helmholtzian physicalist image. Is there any wonder, then, that some of Freud's most basic conceptions (those based on feedforward, programmed control – see Ch. 2) should resemble the reafference theory of Helmholtz and von Holst (1954) while others are developed from feedback (equilibratory) theories such as those of Claude Bernard (1858) that gave rise to the concept of homeostasis.

In short, we strongly feel it is premature if not totally misguided at this juncture of the development of control theory (which is in its infancy) to get rid of energy concepts from psychological theory. We realize that in making this statement we are going against the contemporary *Zeitgeist* which has become dazzled by the profound insights obtained only so recently from information measurement theory and from information processing systems. But it is also true that experimental psychologists have been gravely disappointed with the harvest they have reaped for their science by use in isolation of information theoretic insights (Miller, 1953; Pribram, 1959). None the less, in the words of Ross Ashby (1963, p. 191), 'cybernetic methods may be decisive in the treatment of certain difficult problems not by a direct winning of the solution but by a demonstration that the problem is wrongly conceived, or based on an erroneous assumption'. In fact, the failure in obtaining consistent results when examining information processing channel capacity provided the impetus for a renewed interest in conceptions such as work and effort (see Kahneman, 1973, Ch. 1 for a succinct summary). We thus hope that by clearly distinguishing between information and energy concepts and by pointing the directions in which control theory can be developed and applied, we can help establish a more balanced climate of inquiry which prevents both over-enthusiastic application of new insights to inappropriate content, and throwing out the baby with the bathwater. However, in agreement with McFarland, we emphasize that energy concepts used causally rather than functionally can give rise to many misconceptions. Thus, as will be developed, we do not subscribe to Freud's use of Q, of 'energy', in the form of neurochemical excitation as a simple 'driving force' (*Triebefeder*). However, we will retain such concepts as 'effort' in describing the associative and dissociative processes among neural and behavioural systems. In short, Freud's regulatory principles are in some instances wrong when viewed from the vantage of contemporary control theory. And they need to be re-examined and modified in the light of current neurophysiology as well. However, the regulatory principles are meant to detail mechanisms of control and so are clearly amenable to such re-examination and modification.

Within such a framework it becomes clear that the regulatory principles enunciated in the *Project*, and developed in the psychoanalytic literature thereafter, deal with constraints among interacting systems each of which tends to conserve its equilibrium. This is the unitary mechanism of inertia. However, beyond this recognition of their root commonality each regulatory principle must not only be examined for validity with respect to the data base which produced the principle but also from the vantage of contemporary control theory to provide hypotheses for new inquiry. In the remainder of this and in following chapters we initiate such examinations.

PRIMARY AND SECONDARY PROCESSES

The essence of the distinction between primary and secondary neural function is, as we saw in the quotation on page 29, that primary functions lead to *discharge* of excitation while secondary functions lead to specific actions by virtue of a *constant* quantity of energy. This elementary relationship becomes developed into the concepts primary (this chapter) and secondary processes (see Ch. 2) so important in later psychoanalytic thought. We need therefore to look into this fundamental distinction in some detail.

Our point of departure is an analysis of what is meant by 'discharge' which is often taken as the characteristic of primary processes as well as of primary function. We will maintain and document that to dispose of primary processes in this fashion is an oversimplification which leads to an impoverished view of the psychological process. In the *Project*, discharge refers to *neural* discharge and is manifest in *three* separate ways: one route is through the motor systems, a second is through discharge to neighbouring neural systems, and a third is through biochemical systems. Each of these routes of discharge is capable of involving critical feedback: the 'motor' route elicits social consequences (see below); the 'neural' route involves the cortico-subcortical feedbacks of attention (see Ch. 3); and the 'biochemical' route produces 'unpleasure' by activating other circulating chemicals to which the brain is sensitive (see 'Drives', this chapter). We will take up here the motor and some of the simpler aspects of the neighbouring neural routes, leaving the biochemical to the next section of this chapter.

The motor paths of discharge are mentioned repeatedly:

These neurones must have a discharge, however small, . . . [*which*] will, like all others, go in the direction of motility. . . .

(S.E., p. 311)

Again:

The quantity of the . . . stimulus excites the nervous system's trend to discharge, by transforming itself into a proportionate motor excitation. . . . The quantities which are translated in this way produce an effect far superior quantitatively to themselves, by entering the muscles, glands, etc., – acting there, that is, by a *release* [of quantity], whereas between neurones only a *transference* takes place.

(S.E., p. 314)

This paragraph might suggest that the simple transfer of excitation between neurons is not to be classified as a primary process. This is definitely not so. Even though release through the motor systems is not involved, *discharge* of one neuron onto neighbouring ones can be part of a primary process. Thus,

In these two cases we must no doubt see the *primary process* in respect of judging, and we may assume that all secondary judging has come about through a mitigation *of these purely associative processes* [*italics ours*].

Further: (S.E., pp. 333-4)

. . . It [*thought*] must make no essential change in the facilitations created by the primary processes. . . .

(S.E., p. 335)

The real issue in making the distinction between primary and secondary processes thus does not rest on the basis of 'motor release of quantity'. Rather, the issue is whether quantity is transferred or held more or less constant in the service of a specific action:

Thus the secondary process is a repetition of the original . . . passage [of quantity], *at a lower level, with smaller quantities.*

(S.E., p. 334)

Again, one might be misled by this quotation into thinking that the transfer of large quantities is the *sine qua non* of the primary-secondary process distinction. But reading on in the *Project* one is quickly disabused of this idea for the next section is entitled 'Primary Processes – Sleep and Dreams'. Here, as in the above quotation on judging, *associative* mechanisms are invoked as definitive of primary processes which are here at play without any transfer of large quantities of excitation:

It is an important fact that . . . *primary processes,* . . . are daily presented to us during sleep . . . the precondition [*for which*] is a *lowering of the endogenous load in the* [*nuclear neurons*], which makes the secondary function superfluous.

(S.E., p. 336)

The distinction between large quantities of energy and smaller quantities is frequently and, on the basis of the above quotations, we believe erroneously made the basis of the relationship between the primary and secondary processes. The distinction is described as the relationship between energy or power engineering and information engineering. Rapaport has already suggested the error of this view in a review of Norbert Wiener's book on cybernetics (1948) and adds:

The student of ego-psychology will probably feel that this is not simply a matter of the power-engineering of the drives *or* of the communication engineering of the secondary process and the ego, but rather one of the complex process . . . which makes the dynamics of thought (experimental action) a combination of power- and communication-engineering . . . 'in the flesh' information and communication arises only when *motivation* for it is present.

(Rapaport, 1950 b)

Rapaport makes other points about the relationship between information and communication theory on the one hand and the psychoanalytic metapsychology on the other, and as we have already noted, Peterfreund has devoted an entire monograph to this issue. And we are in this volume attempting to bring to bear aspects of control theory that have hitherto been ignored. Since we insist that energy concepts in psychology are to be used as they are in physics, i.e. they are to be derived functionally rather than invoked causally, so we also take exception to the idea that motivation can be understood in terms of power engineering concepts while secondary processes are to be understood in terms of communication theory. As we will see (Ch. 2), in the *Project*, motivation is based on memory conceived of as facilitated neural pathways which are controlled by others, inhibitory in function. The memory-motive structures, although the basis for secondary processes, are in themselves primary process mechanisms. Only when the inhibitory controls are operative is the process secondary. We suggest, therefore, that information processing concepts are especially relevant to the development of secondary cognitive functions (as detailed in Chs. 2 and 3) but are not *pari-passu* identical with them.

As we see it, in keeping with the view of control theory presented earlier in the chapter, the distinction between primary and secondary processes can be made to rest on the following: primary processes are those which result in an increase or decrease in the energy (capacity for work) of the systems involved (see Ch. 5 for mechanisms). Thus primary processes take place when *associative transfer* (or discharge) occurs between neurons (or between neurons and effectors). By contrast, secondary processes are those in which the capacity for work (change) of the systems under consideration remains constant (and usually high). Secondary processes almost always concern the organization of specific actions with regard to endogenous excitations and environmental exigencies by means of more complexly structured *cognitive mechanisms*. The distinction between association and cognition

40

is made repeatedly in the *Project* in discussions that contrast primary and secondary processes:

The connections in dreams are partly *nonsensical*, partly *feeble-minded*, or even meaningless or strangely crazy.
  This latter characteristic is explained by the fact that in dreams the *compulsion to associate* prevails. . . .

(S.E., p. 338)

And again:

Thus judging, which is later a means for *cognition* of an object . . . is originally an *associative* [*italics ours*] process. . . .

(S.E., p. 334)

We return to this distinction between associative and cognitive mechanisms toward the end of this chapter and at still greater length in Chapters 4 and 5. But in order to grasp the elaborate neurophysiological detail of the secondary process presented in the *Project*, we must first turn to the remaining form of primary function, drives, conceived not only as internal stimuli but as a brain mechanism akin to 'a sympathetic ganglion' and thus a discharge into a biochemical system.

DRIVES

In the *Project* control of behaviour lies in the way in which the nervous system processes its inputs, both those derived from within the organism and those from the outside, i.e. the environment. A central theme in Freud's writings, as well as in the explications of his model by others, deals with the relative emphasis to be placed on the factors impinging from without and from within – and with their relationship to each other. It is pretty well accepted (e.g. Strachey, S.E., vol. 1, pp. 291–2; see quote below) that in psychoanalytic theory there was an initial period in which Freud was essentially an environmentalist; that this was succeeded by a period during which he discovered that he had been wrong in taking at face value his patients' reports of seductions, and so developed the idea of instinctual drive – thus coming, for quite a period of time, to devote his major attention to internal factors. The belief is that only subsequently was this improper emphasis redressed by Freud's rediscovery of the role of the external environment, and particularly of the ego as the organ of adaptation:

This brings us to another major difference between Freud's theories in the *Project* and his later ones. All the emphasis in the picture here is upon the environment's impact upon the organism and the organism's reaction to it. It is true that, in addition to external stimuli, there are endogenous excitations; but their nature is hardly considered. The 'instincts' are only shadowy entities, with scarcely even a name. The interest in the endogenous excitations is restricted in the main to 'defensive' operations and their mechanisms. It is a curious fact that what was later to be the almost omnipotent 'pleasure principle' is here regarded solely as an inhibiting mechanism. Indeed, even in *The Interpretation of Dreams*, published four years later, it is still always called the 'unpleasure principle'. Internal forces are scarcely more than secondary reactions to external ones. The id, in fact, is still to be discovered.

Bearing this in mind, we can perhaps arrive at a more general view of the development of Freud's theories. What we have in the *Project* is a pre-id – a 'defensive' – description of the mind. With the recognition of infantile sexuality and the analysis of the sexual instincts Freud's interests were diverted from defence and for some twenty years he devoted himself largely to the study of the id. It was only when that study seemed more or less exhausted that he returned, in the last period of his work, to a consideration of defence. It has often been pointed out that it is in the *Project* that we can find a foretaste of the structural ego which emerges in *The Ego and the Id*. But this is quite naturally so. There were bound to be similarities between a pre-id and a post-id picture of psychological processes.

(S.E., Editor's Introduction, pp. 291–2)

One of our purposes will be to show that this historical estimate of Freud's position is to some extent incorrect, as has also been pointed out recently by Kanzer (1973). It does have a germ of truth, but at the same time it underplays the role which Freud from the *very beginning* ascribed to a balance between the factors from the environment, especially those produced by the caretaking person during infancy, and those from within – and even specifically to instinctual drives.

As already noted, when organisms become complex, they do not derive all (or even a major part) of their excitation through transactions with the external environment. At least equally important are the 'forces from within' – neural excitations derived from what Freud calls 'endogenous stimuli'. Not only are *quantities* produced from the operation of endogenous processes; the *qualities* of pleasure and unpleasure (German: *Unlust*) are also derived from these sources.

With an [increasing] complexity of the interior [of the organism], the nervous system receives stimuli from the somatic element itself – endogenous stimuli – which have equally to be discharged. These have their origin in the cells of the body and give rise to the major needs: hunger, respiration, sexuality.

(S.E., pp. 296–7)

Freud ascribes a principal role to these endogenous stimuli from the very start: he makes them the essential input to a major portion of the neural apparatus to which he attaches the letter ψ, psi, for psychological, since he feels that this is the most interesting system for (clinical) psychology. (This intimate connection between endogenous stimulation and ψ is contrasted with an equally intimate connection between exogenous input through pathways called ϕ, phi – for peripheral – and the cerebral cortex, labelled ω, omega, for *Warnehmung* – German for awareness.) Psi is described thus:

The primary brain fits pretty well with our characterization of the system ψ, if we may assume that paths lead directly, and independently of ϕ [*the exogenous input pathways*], from the brain to the interior of the body. Now, the derivation and original biological significance of the primary brain, are not known to anatomists; according to our theory, it would, to put it plainly, be a *sympathetic ganglion*. Here is a first possibility of testing our theory upon factual material.

(S.E., p. 303)

How well has the theory survived such tests? Recent advances in neurochemistry have, in fact, demonstrated a host of brain systems akin to 'sympathetic ganglia' in the sense that the neurohumours secreted are amines closely related to those produced by such ganglia. These catecholamines (noradrenalin and dopamine) and near relatives the indole amines (e.g. seratonin) are now known to regulate mood and sleep-activity cycles, although the specific mechanisms as to which neurohumour produces what effect and when are still in question and under investigation. Again, we propose that we examine the basic concept as it appears in the *Project* in light of today's neurochemical findings to see how that concept relates to current knowledge and then develop a more appropriate version.

If this [*view of ψ as a sympathetic ganglion*] is so, however, ψ is exposed to Qs on this side without protection and in this fact lies the *mainspring* of the psychical mechanism.

(S.E., pp. 315–16)

Again,

Here ψ is at the mercy of Q, and it is thus that in the interior of the system there arises the impulsion which sustains all psychical activity. . . . We know this power as the *will* – the derivative of the *instincts* [*more appropriately translated as 'drives' since the original uses the term 'Triebe'*].

(S.E., p. 317)

So we already have the introduction of the term '*Triebe*', the word that Freud used throughout his work for what is translated into English as 'instinct'. This translation, as many others, is unfortunate. As noted earlier, von Holst and Mittelstaedt (1950) in their classic studies on instinctive behaviours of insects have shown these in large part to consist of feedforward, while as noted here, the mechanisms of drive are basically feedback processes. More recently, Mayr (1961, 1971) has reviewed the entire problem. He develops the suggestion that instincts, i.e. genetically determined behaviour patterns, are teleonomic and not teleologic (Pittendrigh's distinction, 1958) in that they are programmed (and thus feedforward). Similar considerations led Waddington (1957) to distinguish homeorhetic processes from homeostatic, and Pribram (1960, 1971) to suggest that homeorhesis is accomplished through a biasing, feedforward resetting of homeostatic controls.

But the organization of drives, as portrayed in the *Project*, though primarily feedback processes, are also subject to adaptive regulation. Discharge of ψ stimulation can be effected through a variety of pathways. According to Freud's model, one of these paths leads to the interior of the body via 'key' secretory neurons which produce chemical substances. These impinge on target areas that in turn add more chemical substances which cause even more excitation of the endogenous paths of conduction. In terms of today's control theory this loop, once activated, consists of a positive feedback mechanism, which, if there were no way to stop it, would lead to an ever increasing accrual of excitation. Here is Freud's statement of this fundamental conception:

Just as there are motor neurones which, when they are filled to a certain amount, conduct $Q\overset{\ast}{\eta}$ into the muscles and accordingly discharge it, so there must be 'secretory' neurones which, when they are excited, cause the generation in the interior of the body of something which operates as a stimulus upon the endogenous paths of conduction to ψ – neurones which thus influence the production of endogenous $Q\overset{\ast}{\eta}$, and accordingly do not discharge $Q\overset{\ast}{\eta}$ but supply it in roundabout ways. We will call these [secretory] neurones 'key neurones'. Evidently they are only excited when a certain level in ψ has been reached.

(S.E., pp. 320–21)

And what are these endogenous stimuli? Freud conceives them to be chemical:

. . . a suspicion forces itself on us that . . . the endogenous stimuli consist of *chemical products*, of which there may be a considerable number.

(S.E., p. 321)

A word about the historical context in which Freud developed this rather complicated mechanism of drive and drive control. Meynert, Freud's revered teacher, in his *Vorlesungen über Psychiatrie* (1890), had argued that functional hyperemia of the brain is felt as pleasurable and anemic conditions of the brain as reverse. The central neurons were presumed to 'perceive' their own nutritive conditions. From this it is but a step to neurons which sense chemical substances.

What we know of the *endogenous* stimuli may be expressed in the assumption that they are of an intercellular nature, that they arise continuously and only periodically become psychical stimuli.

(S.E., p. 316)

Recent experiments have amplified and specified the receptor functions of neural tissue located in the core parts of the neuraxis: one of us has reviewed elsewhere (Pribram, 1960, 1971) the evidence that such central sensitivities exist – receptors sensitive to the partial pressure of CO_2 (respiration), glucose (hunger), and osmotic concentration (thirst), estrogens (sex) and temperature have been located.

The conception of key neurons, the effector end of the positive feedback loop, has been more difficult to trace. Most likely, Freud was acquainted with the well known experiments of Sechenov (1863; English edn 1965) who used chemical excitation of the roof of the mesencephalon to produce changes in movements reflexly produced by stimulation of the skin. Also, there existed considerable controversy concerned with whether diabetes insipidus was caused by hypothalamic or pituitary inadequacy (E. Pribram, thesis, personal communication). The role of the 'ductless glands' in secreting hormones was being actively investigated even then and we do know today of a whole series of neuroendocrine substances of hypothalamic origin which act as releasers for the various pituitary hormones – among others, ACTH releaser would make a good candidate for one of Freud's substances which would 'introduce' quantity 'in roundabout ways'.

Yet it is just at this point that contemporary control theory and neurophysiological research place Freud's theory somewhat in jeopardy. Ever since Cannon's (1927, 1929) classic contributions, neurochemical and neuroendocrine processes have been thought of as consisting primarily of homeostatic, which are negative, not positive feedback mechanisms. This is a fundamental difference. Only when such mechanisms get out of control, when the timing of the feedback becomes misaligned, do oscillations and disruptions resulting from positive feedback occur. It should be pointed out that this effect of timing has

45

rarely been considered, either at the neurophysiological level (where technical difficulties impede investigation) or at the behavioural level.

Another consideration has been added by the discovery of the activating functions of the mesencephalic reticular formation which is the locus for many of the special sensitivities to brain amines (Lindsley, 1961; Magoun, 1958). Such activation can be conceptualized to alter the set points, that is the point at which homeostatic negative feedback mechanisms are set to operate (Pribram, 1960, 1971) much as our home thermostats can be set to operate at a certain level by turning a small wheel which adjusts the separation of the metal sensors that act to switch the heater on and off. With one major difference, a feedback mechanism with a tunable, that is biasable, set point would behave not altogether differently from that portrayed in the *Project*. Feedback control with set point has the critical advantage, however, that *deficient* stimulation as well as excessive is adjusted to. In the light of this more modern view of the mechanism, the emphasis in the *Project* and in later psychiatric literature on the overriding importance of discharge as the ultimate mechanism for restituting equilibrium is untenable and must be abandoned. In its place, we propose that any change in set point, or any change in the equilibration of the systems will produce an initial arousal followed by a process which 'readies' the organism to cope with this and similar disturbances of equilibrium that may recur. For details of the evidence for this two-step process see Pribram and McGuinness (1975, Parts I and II).

In yet another instance psychology can benefit from study of the *Project*. It is in the regulation of neurochemical drive processes that the *Project* spells out the details of a mechanism by which internal change serves the adaptive function of relating to other human beings, in other words, how drive and drive gratification become integrated in an interpersonal context. In this early statement, Freud is convincingly clear:

The filling of the nuclear neurones in ψ will have as its result an effort to discharge, an *urgency* which is released along the motor pathway. Experience shows that here the first path to be taken is that leading to *internal change* (expression of the emotions, screaming, vascular innervation). But, as was explained at the beginning [p. 297], no such discharge can produce an unburdening result, since the endogenous stimulus continues to be received and the ψ tension is restored. The removal of the stimulus is only made possible here by an intervention which for the time being gets rid of the release of $Q\dot{\eta}$ in the interior of the body; and this intervention calls for an alteration in the external world (supply of nourishment, proximity of the sexual object) which, as a *specific action*, can only be brought about in definite ways. At first, the human organism is incapable of bringing about the specific action. It takes place by *extraneous help*, when the attention of an experienced person is drawn to the child's state by discharge along the path of internal change. In this way this path of discharge acquires a secondary function of the highest importance, that of *communication*, and the initial helplessness of human beings is the *primal source* of all *moral motives*.

(S.E., pp. 317–18)

This early and intimate organizational meshing of instinctual-drive processes with those that are the source of all moral, i.e. interpersonal motives, later internalized as superego functions, was temporarily de-emphasized when attention was focused on one and then the other of these intertwined aspects of the psychic apparatus. Gill (1963, p. 146) has recently, in attempting to clarify current definitions of ego and id, proposed the following:

The last two definitions which I have proposed have the advantage of conceptualizing drive and drive restraints as functionally inseparable and as aspects of behavior. . . . From the arguments presented in this monograph, I believe that it is better to conceptualize the organization of drive, drive restraint and drive discharge together.

Obviously, in his initial formulation of the psychoanalytic model, Freud also conceived of drive, drive restraint and drive gratification as mutually influencing operations that involve the organization of structures developing in the brain.

With the progressive specialization of neurological and behavioural scientists this very primitive and early meshing of an environmentally modulated mechanism of regulation of internal stimulation has often been lost sight of, leading to separate schools of thought: environmentalists who tend to ignore individual differences in sensitivity and capacity that predispose to one or another psychological or behavioural reaction; and organicists who tend to ignore the fact that the structures they want to treat have been formed and transformed by individual experience and that they must therefore take into account that experience. We now know that even the visual system will not develop properly when deprived of adequate stimulation during a sensitive period of development (Riesen, 1970); we also know that we can modify the selectivity of cells in the visual system during this period (Hirsch and Spinelli, 1970; Blakemore, 1974). In short, neural structure is modifiable by experience and is therefore sensitive to the vicissitudes

47

of the environment both external and internal and the timing of their coincidence. The *Project* is specific in detail as to how the neural structures that regulate behaviour – i.e. the organism's motivational structures – come to be. But before we can turn to these structures – the detailed model presented in the *Project* – we must take note of some other paradoxical processes of discharge – processes which are paradoxical because discharge increases rather than decreases the total amount of excitation in the nervous system.

PAIN AND UNPLEASURE

Due to the complex organization of neural interconnections (and their feedback characteristics) the tendency of the neural apparatus towards total and immediate discharge is even in the *Project* considered to be untenable. However, since discharge does play a role in the manifestation of drive, as already discussed, an activating process was posited. This mechanism is also invoked to explain psychological pain, unpleasure, wish and affect. These processes are all considered to temporarily augment excitation within the nervous system and are therefore primary in the sense that an associative transfer between neurons occurs. Thus, they are considered the possible occasions for the development of pathological processes by Freud. Let us follow his argument.

All contrivances of a biological nature have limits to their efficiency, beyond which they fail. This failure is manifested in phenomena which border on the pathological – which might be described as normal prototypes of the pathological. We have found that the nervous system is contrived in such a way that the major external Qs are kept off from ϕ and still more from ψ: [by] the nerve-ending screens, [and by] the merely indirect connection between ψ and the external world. Is there a phenomenon which can be brought to coincide with the failure of these contrivances? Such, I think, is *pain*.

(S.E., pp. 306–7)

The exciting cause of pain may be just an increase in quantity; all sensory excitations tend to turn into pain if stimulation is increased beyond a certain point. Pain may also occur, however, when the external excitations are small: when this is so it is regularly associated with a 'breach in continuity: that is, an external Q which acts directly on the ends of the ϕ neurons and not through the nerve-ending apparatuses produces pain' (p. 307). But more often, it is when the *memory* traces (see Ch. 2) of a pain-producing occurrence are in any manner triggered. Then

... a state arises which is not pain but which nevertheless has a resemblance to it. It includes unpleasure and the inclination to discharge which corresponds to the experience of pain. Since unpleasure signifies a rise in level, it must be asked where this $Q\dot{\eta}$ comes from.

(S.E., p. 320)

Since unpleasure is most usually due to the activation of a memory trace of a painful occurrence, the only quantity initially available is contained in that memory trace,

... and it is clear that this is in the nature of any other perception and cannot have as a result a general raising of $Q\dot{\eta}$.

It only remains to assume, therefore, that owing to the cathexis of memories unpleasure is *released* from the interior of the body and freshly conveyed up.

(S.E., p. 320)

Freud uses the phrase 'release of unpleasure' or the 'generation of unpleasure' as shorthand descriptions that denote the production of chemical substances. These in turn lead, by way of the drive mechanism, to an increase in intercellular chemicals in the brain. This whole process can (or may fail to) be reflected in an increase in quantity in that subdivision of the brain involved in perception (see Ch. 3), and thus be *perceived* as unpleasant:

We cannot avoid the idea that there is an accumulation; and the intermittant character of their psychical effect [*i.e. the effect of the endogenous excitations*] necessitates the view that on their path of conduction to ψ they come up against resistances which are overcome only when there is an increase in quantity. ... Above a certain Q, however, they [the endogenous excitations] act as a stimulus continuously, and every increase of Q is perceived as an increase of the ψ stimulus. It follows, therefore, that there is a state in which the path of conduction has become permeable. Experience shows, further, that, after the ψ stimulus has been discharged, the path of conduction resumes its resistance once more.

(S.E., p. 316)

Note that drive stimuli, endogenous substances can, but need not necessarily, produce the perception of unpleasure and that perception depends on *quantity*. Here perhaps more than anywhere else in the *Project*, Freud feels he has an unsolved problem (see Freud, 1954, p. 176) and our analysis based on current data comes to a rather different view. In the terms of the *Project*, Freud should have recognized that both pain and unpleasure are 'qualitative' not 'quantitative' conceptions since they are *perceived* in consciousness. Therefore, by his own thesis, some *pattern* (measurable in terms of quality or information) or *lack of pattern* must be responsible for the perceptions of pain and unpleasure – a 'quantitative' energy explanation is out of place. Freud in fact recognized this but only belatedly. His last comments on 'pleasure' in *An Outline of Psycho-Analysis* explicitly make the point:

The raising of tensions is in general felt as *unpleasure* and their lowering as *pleasure*. It is probable, however, that what is felt as pleasure or unpleasure is not the *absolute* height of this tension but something in the rhythm of the changes in them.

(S.E., vol. 23, p. 146)

Had Freud, from the beginning, kept clearly separate his concept of drive from that of unpleasure (and therefore pleasure) – with drive the quantitative, and unpleasure the qualitative concept – we should have been spared many confusions in later writings. Rapaport (1961), for instance, has had to call attention to the fact that the *mechanism* of pleasure-unpleasure has nothing necessarily to do with the *perception* of pleasure or unpleasure.

Further, explanations in terms of patterning in pain and unpleasure would have left the way open for incorporating the results of subsequent research (see e.g. the research by Albe-Fessard and Kruger, 1962; Kruger and Michel, 1962; Kruger, Siminoff and Witkovsky, 1961) on the neural nature of pain and its control (e.g. Melzack and Wall, 1965) as well as the sensitivities of these mechanisms to neuropharmacological substances (Liebeskind, Mayer and Akil, 1974). These experiments detail that any neuron that can be excited by a painful stimulus (e.g. tooth pulp irritation) is also excited by touch, pressure or proprioceptive manipulations. A control process based on a negative feedback mechanism at the spinal cord level has therefore been proposed. When that control is exercised by *patterned* stimulation from somatosensory receptors, touch, pressure, etc., are perceived; when uncontrolled positive feedback produces oscillatory and disruptive stimulation, unpatterned pain is perceived. Thus Freud was partially correct: an increase in quantity *disrupts* pattern and this unpatterned excitation is perceived as pain. However, conscious awareness of pain, as is the case elsewhere, is dependent on the dimension of pattern – the lack of pattern in this case.

Brainstem mechanisms (periaqueductal grey) have also been shown by electrical stimulation (though not by excision of this tissue) to produce control over pain and the cells involved are the locus of the analgesic action of morphine. In short, pain and unpleasure can be broken up by patterned somatosensory input which leads to the inference that pain is produced in the absence of, or by the overwhelming of such patterned input. Pain is also controlled by brainstem stimulation of sites chemically sensitive to at least one potent analgesic and producer of euphoria – morphine.

In summary, study of the mechanisms of drive, pain and unpleasure as presented in the *Project* and analysis of the problems presented demand revision of current psychoanalytic conceptions regarding the role of 'instinctual drives' as mechanisms regulating behaviour. Contemporary neuropsychology, neurophysiology and control theory provides a rich source of data. These refute some of the proposals put forth in the *Project*. Thus the allegation so often levied, that Freud's theories are untestable, is shown to be incorrect. In addition, we find in the *Project* a concise statement of the *problems* to be investigated, problems as current today as they were in 1895.

AFFECT

Affect 'is brought about . . . by sudden release' (S.E., p. 322) of previously stored excitation 'by facilitation': a new experience activates a set of neural memory traces (see Ch. 2) often, but not invariably sufficient to activate the pathway leading either to major motor or key neuron discharge pathways. When these pathways do not become involved but the discharge reaches the cortex the affect may serve as a signal. In either case the stored excitations are thus explosively liberated (as, by analogy, when a condensor discharges).

These have in common the fact that they both involve a raising of $Q\dot{\eta}$ tension in ψ – brought about in the case of an *affect* by sudden release and in that of a *wish* [*see below*] by summation.

(S.E., p. 322)

Obviously, the discharge theory of affects of *The Interpretation of Dreams* (S.E., vol. 5, p. 582) and of the metapsychological papers is already present in the *Project*.

One question puzzled us considerably. Stated succinctly the query reads: 'Is affect always negative for Freud?' If it were, what then is the difference between affect and unpleasure? We did not satisfy ourselves on this point until we realized that, in Freud's definition, affect *per se* is neither negative nor positive but can only lead to pleasurable or unpleasurable *consequences*. Thus the *Project* already contains explicitly the concept of the signal value of affect: whenever a set of memory traces is activated and initiates a facilitation which liberates previously bound excitations, affect results. But then the *Project* reverts to a quantitative view of the pleasure-unpleasure process, which, as we have seen, is logically confusing and neurologically untenable.

Nevertheless, this early conception suggests that affect can lead to either pleasure or unpleasure. Because the early theory dealt so heavily with pathological states, and hence with defence against unpleasure, it seems to have stressed those conditions which lead to unpleasure. The very definition of affect we quoted from the *Project* dealt with the reproduction of an experience of pain. But we must recall also that it is sexual affect with which the theory largely dealt, that such affect presumably leads to pleasure in non-pathological conditions. In fact, the problem of change from pleasure to unpleasure was felt by Freud to be at the heart of the problem of repression. It is in this connection that he explicitly – though incidentally and in a hypothesis about dreams – did define the pleasurable results of affect in the *Project*:

> . . . the release of pleasure . . . is slight, because in general they [*dreams*] run their course almost without affect (without motor release). (S.E., p. 340)

As already noted, a major reason for confusion in historical assessments of the role of drives in Freud's writings has been a misunderstanding of the varieties of neural processes that are postulated to result in activation, the augmentation of excitation. Confusion between the processes denoted by the term 'affect' and the term 'drive' has been especially troubling. It is felt by some that Freud's term for the basic 'psychic force' was 'affect' rather than 'drive'. The principal justifications for this are first, the crucial passage in which Freud seems to define 'sum of excitation' as 'affect', that is to say, to equate these two terms; and second, the theory of abreaction, which describes the quantity that had to be abreacted as an affect. Let us first inquire into the conclusion that 'sum of excitation' and 'affect' are the same. Rapaport (1953), for example, bases himself heavily on this passage by Freud:

> I should like finally, to dwell for a moment on the working hypothesis which I have made use of in this exposition of the neuroses of defence. I refer to the concept that in mental functions something is to be distinguished – *a quota of affect* [*emphasis ours*] or sum of excitation – which possesses all the characteristics of a quantity (though we have no means of measuring it), which is capable of increase, diminution, displacement and discharge, and which is

spread over the memory-traces of ideas somewhat as an electric charge is spread over the surface of a body.

(*The Neuro-Psychoses of Defence,*
S.E., vol. 3, p. 60)

Strachey argues that the equation of 'sum of excitation' and 'quota of affect' is incorrect, in the sense that Freud did not mean that all sums of excitation were to be called affect, but only that affect is a particular kind of sum of excitation. Strachey's discussion, in an appendix to *The Neuro-Psychoses of Defence* (vol. 3, p. 68), makes the following suggestion: what seems to be evidence equating 'quota of affect' with 'sum of excitation' is Freud's definition of 'quota of affect' in his paper, *Repression* (1915). This definition states that affect is the quantitative factor in the representation of drive. Strachey points out that in the very same passage Freud 'mentions as a possible instinctual vicissitude "the transformation into affects . . . of the psychical energies of [*drives*]." ' Strachey concludes: 'It is probably correct to suppose that Freud was regarding the "quota of affect" as a particular manifestation of the "sum of excitation".'

We agree with Strachey's position (since, as we will show shortly, wish is another such manifestation) and would like to suggest that the *Project* contains the sought-for clarification. As detailed in the sections on drive and unpleasure, secretions from key neurons do in fact produce activation, a positive feedback that 'transforms' drive into a 'sum of excitation' in the ψ system. In short, affect is initiated by environmental stimulations but supported and augmented by the resulting endogenous excitation. An affect is precipitated suddenly by the environmental activation of a memory that is charged with an endogenously originating load.

With this definition from the *Project* in mind let us see whether, using it, we can clarify the considerable confusion that now exists in psychoanalysis regarding affect. A seeming confusion in Freud's first paper on anxiety neurosis (1895), written shortly before the *Project*, is a case in point.

Why, under such conditions of psychical insufficiency in mastering sexual excitation, does the nervous system find itself in the peculiar affective state of *anxiety*? An answer may be suggested as follows. The psyche finds itself in the *affect* of anxiety if it feels unable to deal by appropriate reaction with a task (a danger) *approaching from outside*; it finds itself in the *neurosis* of anxiety if it notices that it is unable to even out the (sexual) excitation originating *from within* – that is to say, *it behaves as though it were projecting that excitation outward*. The affect and its corresponding neurosis are firmly related to each

53

other. The first is a reaction to an exogenous excitation, the second a reaction to the analogous endogenous one. The affect is a state which passes rapidly, the neurosis is a chronic one; because, while exogenous excitation operates with a single impact, the endogenous excitation operates as a constant force. *In the neurosis, the nervous system is reacting against a source of excitation which is internal, whereas in the corresponding affect it is reacting against an analogous source of excitation which is external.*

(S.E., vol. 3, p. 112)

Freud here is distinguishing between neurosis and affect in the same way in which he distinguishes between drive and exogenous stimulus. He seems to be saying that neurosis is equivalent to drive and affect is equivalent to exogenous stimulus. But note that affect is not the exogenous stimulation *per se* but a memory-based *reaction* to the excitations derived from exogenous sources; so affect is defined just as it was in the *Project*, namely, as initiated in a memory and 'a state which passes rapidly'. And similarly, neurosis (an overriding wish, see below) is not equivalent to drive but is a memory-based *reaction* to drive – i.e. to the excitations derived from endogenous sources. (It is incidentally worth noting that in 1895 Freud was already writing about anxiety aroused by a danger approaching from the outside, a formulation which does not return in similar fashion until *Inhibitions, Symptoms and Anxiety* in 1926.)

The second reason some regard affect, rather than drive, '*Triebe*', to be the prime motive force, '*Antrieb*', is that it is affect which must be abreacted according to the cathartic theory of therapy. It is true that Freud suggested in this theory that affect was the result of a traumatic experience which was not adequately worked over and discharged. So one might again conclude that the affect is derived exclusively from external stimulation. But again it must be emphasized that Freud's view does not hold that the experience introduces the quantity which is to be released as affect. Rather, the experience incites the activation – potential affect becomes actual.

In the very earliest stages of his cathartic theory, Freud did not mention the source of quantity for this affect. That he thought it to originate from within, even in that period during which he believed in the tales of seduction, is demonstrated by his hypothesis of the greatly increased discharge of affect after puberty (in contrast to the amount which was released at the time that the alleged seduction first took place). Of course, in the *later* development of the psychoanalytic theory of affect, it came, as we already noted, to be described as the quantitative representative of drive, and hence was much more closely equated with the drive concept. In the earlier theory, as stated in the *Project*, the initiation of affect by external experience was stressed, though endogenous excitation already played a dominant role in determining its amount and duration. The later theory of affect then seems to us to be one more expression of the manner in which, during the period of the metapsychological papers, the proper balance between external and internal had become skewed – as a consequence of Freud's having burned his fingers with the seduction hypothesis – and the resulting emphasis on the exploration of the drives in favour of the internal as against the external.

WISH AND WILL:
A PRIMARY–SECONDARY PROCESS DISTINCTION

According to the theory outlined in the *Project* wishful states also result from the activation of memory traces; they differ from unpleasure in that wishing (p. 319) is a 'state of urgency' produced by the activation of memory traces of *pleasurable* experiences that supervene and bring relief from tension; and from affect in that they accrue gradually 'by summation', as noted in the quotation at the beginning of the section on affect. Thus memory images involved in a pleasurable experience are those that originally were responsible for the relief of increased tension: viz. those associated with the organism's own tension releasing *movements* and those that represent the occasion (or object) on which depended the tension release (p. 319).

The emergence of another object in place of the hostile one was the signal for the fact that the experience of pain was at an end, and the ψ system, taught *biologically*, seeks to reproduce the state in ψ which marked the cessation of pain.

(S.E., p. 322)

This 'seeking to reproduce the state in ψ is called by Freud wishful activation (p. 319) and occurs relatively gradually through a process of summation (p. 322). Activation can on occasion become so powerful that it distorts or even overrides the perceptions initiated by excitations derived directly from the external world (p. 322). We have all experienced the wish to find a loved one in a crowd only to temporarily misidentify every passing similarity. Thus wishful states, initiated by endogenous excitation, become established through summation, and can be augmented through further accrual of endogenous excitation, even to the point of hallucination if the positive feedback mechanism involved in drive and unpleasure is once engaged. For this reason, if discharge is delayed overlong, unpleasure accompanies the wish; if effected relatively quickly, through motor neurons, pleasure results. For this pleasurable affect to endure, however, the discharge must be accomplished in such a fashion that it is appropriate to circumstances which can help prevent the immediate recurrence of the wishful state.

We have already noted the early statement of the relationship between external and internal stimuli as it defines the nature of *affect* and *wish*. This relationship continues to be expressed most explicitly in Freud's later writings about sexual excitation – how sexual wishes and affects are brought about. There is on the one hand the fact that sexual excitation can come about as a result of a building up of excitation from within, sexual drive culminating in wish; and on the other hand, the fact that sexual excitation can also be brought about *more precipitously* by external stimulation either through vision or through an erogenous zone, resulting in what we may define as the sexual affect. This problem is discussed in *Three Essays on the Theory of Sexuality* (1905) in a section called 'The Problem of Sexual Excitation'. Freud first repeats the argument of section three of the first paper on anxiety neurosis by suggesting that

. . . the accumulation of the sexual substances creates and maintains sexual tension; the pressure of these products upon the walls of the vesicles containing them might be supposed to act as a stimulus upon a spinal centre, the condition of which would be perceived by higher centres and would then give rise in consciousness to the familiar sensation of tension. If the excitation of the erotogenic zones increases sexual tension, this could only come about on the supposition that the zones in question are in an anatomical connection that has already been laid down with these centres, that they increase the tonus of the excitation in them, and, if the sexual tension is sufficient, set the sexual act in motion or, if it is insufficient, stimulate the production of the sexual substances.

(*Three Essays*, S.E., vol. 7, p. 213)

Note here once again, that Freud is still concerned with biology, with neurology (spinal and higher centres) and with endocrinology. He proposes, in connection with the discovery of the glands of internal secretion:

It seems probable, then, that special chemical substances are produced in the interstitial portions of the sex-glands; these are then taken up in the blood stream and cause particular parts of the central nervous system to be charged with sexual tension. . . . The question of how sexual excitation arises from the stimulation of erotogenic zones, when the central apparatus has been previously charged, and the question of what interplay arises in the course of these sexual processes between the effects of purely toxic stimuli and the physiological ones – none of this can be treated, even hypothetically, in the present state of our knowledge.

(ibid., p. 215)

Because of the fusion of the drive and affect concepts in the later psychoanalytic writings and the resulting skewing towards a 'drive' bias of theory, Holt (1967) has recently suggested that we redress the balance and turn our attention to wish as a candidate for the prime motive in psychoanalytic formulations:

I propose a 3-stage answer; for everyday clinical use, Freud's old concept of wish; for psychoanalytic theorizing in the immediate future, the model of wishing proposed by Klein (1967); and for ultimate development, a systems conception in terms of which Klein's model will be a microscopic look at one important sector, but only a sector in a larger picture. In the remainder of this paper, I shall expand on each of these proposals.

First, then, wish as a clinical concept. Let me remind you that Freud worked productively for his first 15 years as a psychoanalyst without the concept of *Trieb*, relying primarily on wish as his motivational term. The main dynamic concept in *Studies on Hysteria* – affect-charged, repressed memories – has the major defining properties of wish: it is a cognitive-affective concept, framed in terms of meanings and potentially pleasant or unpleasant outcomes of possible courses of action. The main motivational concept used in the brilliant case history of Dora and in his masterpiece of combined clinical insight and theoretical elaboration, *The Interpretation of Dreams*, is wish. With it he was able to do almost everything that an analyst needs to be able to do with a motivational concept.

Wishes are plainly near cousins to *plans* on one side and to fantasies on the other; they are concrete, often immediately available to introspection, not lofty or vague abstractions. Those who find it hard to shake off reductionistic habits of thought may find these ideas more acceptable if they think of wishes and plans as strictly analogous to the programs of computers.

In an already long paper, I cannot adequately summarize Klein's proposed model of the way wishes may function for those who have not already read his paper 'Peremptory ideation' (1967). It is, I believe, a protoneuro-physiological conception in Rubinstein's sense (1967), in that it describes hypothetical sequences of events in the central nervous system, which are defined by reference to meanings yet are susceptible of being translated into biological terms; it postulates nothing that violates present knowledge in the neurosciences, and draws on some discoveries in these disciplines to supply some postulated processes.

Briefly, Klein diagrams the sequence of events that occur in what he calls a 'cognitive unit of motivation', from the initial desire to the final experience of gratification, as a closed feedback loop. It begins with what he termed a 'region of primary imbalance', an unfortunately vague metaphor implying an unusual state of affairs in one brain region that gives rise to a continuing series of consequences until it is cancelled by an appropriate kind of feedback. As you may recognize, it is basically a translation into modern terminology of Freud's account (in the seventh chapter of *The Interpretation of Dreams*) of the nature of a wish: it begins with 'the excitations produced by internal needs', and ends when 'an "experience of satisfaction" can be achieved which puts an end to the internal stimulus. An essential component of this experience of satisfactions is a particular perception . . . the mnemic image of which remains associated thenceforward with the memory trace of the excitation produced by the need . . . next time this need arises a psychical impulse will at once emerge which will seek to re-cathect the mnemic image of the perception and to re-evoke the perception itself, that is to say, to re-establish the situation of the original satisfaction. An impulse of this kind is what we call a wish' (pp. 565–6). Those who are familiar with 'the Project' of 1895 will recognize a strong and by no means accidental resemblance between this model and Freud's account of what he called judgment, in terms of a wishful cathexis (what might be) and a perceptual cathexis (what exists).

(Holt, 1967, pp. 28–32)

Holt makes these suggestions in keeping with the more cognitive directions that research has led us over the past two decades (e.g. Klein, 1970; Miller, Galanter and Pribram, 1960; Pribram, 1967b, 1971), and the criticisms of causal energy concepts detailed here. However, Holt blurs an essential distinction already present in the *Project*, a distinction of great importance to the development of a coherent cognitive psychology. First:

They [dreams] are *wish-fulfilments* – that is, primary processes following upon experiences of satisfaction [*see Ch. 2*].

(S.E., p. 340)

Then:

Sleep [*as an example of a state in which primary processes are dominant*] is characterized by *motor paralysis (paralysis of the will)*.

(S.E., p. 337)

Wishing is only the primary, willing (intention, Miller, Galanter and Pribram, 1960) the secondary motivational process. We have available in the *Project* and in later cognitive theory the mechanisms of both wish and *will*. As we shall see in Chapter 3, *will* results in specific *action*, an adaptive motor discharge based on complex attentional and judgemental (comparison) processes detailed under the concept reality testing.

Re-examination of the *Project* thus shows a balanced view of the relation between internal and external environment in Freud's first major theoretical statement. It is concretely formulated in a *memory-*based structure of motivation and made explicit in great detail. Let us, therefore, now take a closer look at this memory-motive structure and the structure of ego processes in the *Project*.

[2]

THE STRUCTURE OF MEMORY-MOTIVE AND EGO PROCESSES

NEURON THEORY AND CATHEXIS

We must in this chapter devote some considerable effort to detail the specific neuroanatomical and neurophysiological propositions which make up the early metapsychology. Without this detail, the metapsychology is deprived of its true referents because the second major postulate on which the model is based is neuron theory. Freud initiates his grand design to write a neurological psychology:

The intention is to furnish a psychology that shall be a natural science: that is, to represent psychical processes as quantitatively determinate states of specifiable material particles, thus making those processes perspicuous and free from contradiction. Two principal ideas are involved: [1] What distinguishes activity from rest is to be regarded as Q, subject to the general laws of motion. (2) The neurones are to be taken as the material particles.

(S.E., p. 295)

The neuron is defined as it is today:

... the nervous system consists of distinct and similarly constructed neurones, which have contact with one another through the medium of a foreign substance, which terminate upon one another as they do upon portions of foreign tissue, [and] in which certain lines of conduction are laid down in so far as they [the neurones] receive [excitations] through cell-processes [dendrites] and [give them off] through an axis-cylinder [axon]. They have in addition numerous ramifications of varying calibre.

(S.E., p. 298)

We must recall in this connection that the *Project* was written in 1895, two years before Foster and Sherrington proposed the label 'synapse' for the discontinuities intercalated between the presumed elements that compose the nervous system. Freud used the term 'contact-barriers' to describe these discontinuities. In other respects, the elementary, cellular composition of nervous tissue was assumed essentially as we understand it today – for in 1895 the work of Waldeyer-Hartz (1891) had already been accomplished and published. Freud's statement is in no way as detailed and beautiful a development of neuron theory as that presented by Sherrington (1947) in *The Integrative Action of the Nervous System*. But in one respect, a very important one, neuron theory *à la* Freud is more compatible with current neurophysiological knowledge.

Freud comes to this variant through his desire to combine quantity theory with neuron theory.

The principle of inertia [p. 296] finds its expression in the hypothesis of a *current* passing from the cell's paths of conduction or processes [dendrites] to the axis-cylinder. . . . The secondary function [of the nervous system], however, which calls for the accumulation of $Q\dot{\eta}$ [p. 297], is made possible by the assumption of resistances which oppose discharge; and the structure of neurones makes it probable that the resistances are all to be located in the *contacts* [between one neurone and another], which in this way assume the value of *barriers*.

(S.E., p. 298)

This requirement that quantity be stored, i.e. that excitation is not only transmitted as current but stored in neurons, is central to the development of the model. Freud's German term for this storage of quantity is '*Besetzung*' – 'occupying'. In psychoanalytic English, the translation has been made as 'cathexis' (p. 298) from the Greek *cathedos*, also the base for our word cathode, a negative potential. And today we place great emphasis on the local graded potential changes that can be recorded from nervous tissue (Bishop, 1956; Bullock, 1958; Grey-Walter, 1973; Purpura, 1962; Pribram, 1960, 1971). In more currently acceptable terminology, however, we would consider such changes as 'potentials' resulting from neurochemical processes rather than as 'quantity of energy to be stored up' but the conception is the same. When electrotonic potentials reach a certain magnitude, discharge, an action current, the nerve impulse occurs, and the potential is gradually reconstituted.

At first, we found ourselves incredulous. How could Freud in 1895 anticipate by sixty years an important neurophysiological conceptualization? Especially since this recent view was accomplished only after the results of recording the electrical activity of nervous tissue with newly developed micro and classical macroelectrodes failed in most instances to correlate? Examination of the literature of the turn of the century (e.g. Shäfer's *Textbook of Physiology*, 1900; Exner's *Entwurf*, 1894) shows, however, that graded electrotonic phenomenona were given their due much more then than during the first half of this century. In his *Untersuchungen* (1849), duBois-Reymond had described these local potential (electrotonic) changes of peripheral nerves, and Pflüger in 1859 had just published a comprehensive monograph on the subject. It was only later that the erroneous idea became commonplace that macroelectrode recordings taken from the brain (the EEG) were nothing more than the envelopes of the action currents, impulses 'fired' by a population of cells located under the electrode. (For complete discussion of this problem, see Pribram, 1971, Ch. 1.) Freud thus simply reflected the then current view that important local potential changes, as measured by galvanometers, take place in a nerve without necessarily initiating transmitted impulses. All he had to do was to extrapolate this knowledge to occurrences in the brain.

As already noted (Ch. 1), we therefore take exception to the tone of the conclusions drawn by Strachey in the nature of Q in Appendix C, p. 393 of the Standard Edition (see pp. 32–4).

To repeat, Strachey is correct, of course, in that Freud did not want to identify the basic nature of 'neuronal motion' as electrical. Nor would current neurophysiology. That basic 'motion' must be biochemical and the electrical units are only manifestations of these biochemical events. This does not preclude either Freud or current neurophysiologists from attempts to delineate lawful relations among the electrical events *per se* (e.g. Freud's law of 'association by simultaneity', or today's 'evoked potentials' and unit 'receptive fields').

In contrast to the neuroscientist, the psychoanalytic reader is perhaps not especially surprised by the appearance of the word cathexis, since it is such a common word in metapsychological writing, where it is of course understood to mean energy, *the* basic quantitative term. But, in passing, we note how little attention is paid to the implications of the fact that this is a *neurological* term; a term clearly defined in the *Project* to denote energy, but it is energy *in a particular state in particular neurons*. It is, in fact, sharply distinguished from a quantity in flow (i.e. the nerve impulse). The point is worth dealing with in detail, not merely for its historical value, but also because it will help to clarify the crucial issue of *binding*, to which we will before long turn. We must discuss the ramifications of this nuance because it constitutes the departure point for any further exposition of Freud's neurologically based metapsychology and our attempts at updating.

The distinction between cathexis and current in flow is made very early in the *Project* as one of its central hypotheses:

If we combine this account of the neurones with the conception of the $Q\dot{\eta}$ theory, we arrive at the idea of a *cathected* neurone filled with a certain $Q\dot{\eta}$ while at other times it may be empty. The principle of inertia [p. 296] finds its expression in the hypothesis of a *current* passing from the cell's paths of conduction or processes [dendrites] to the axis-cylinder.

(S.E., p. 298)

Cathexis, then, – and surely the German *Besetzung*, meaning that which occupies or possesses – is appropriate and means the quantity *which fills a neuron*. For the uninitiate it comes as an almost bewildering realization that in this document of 1895 Freud emphasizes the same vital distinction made by contemporary neurophysiology between impulse transmission and graded potential change, the first referring to rapid discharge along a nerve and the other referring to slow changes in potential differences in the nervous tissue, especially its dendritic portions. The basic distinction is that between a quantity of excitation which moves rapidly along the axon – the usual nerve impulse discharge phenomenon – and a cathexis which is a quantity that is held in the neurons, biases (tunes) their activity, and is usually related to the dendrites. The understanding of this meaning of cathexis is vital to at least three major issues of Freud's model. One of these is the emergence of consciousness. Freud wrote:

It should further be suspected that an intense current of $Q\dot{\eta}$ is not favourable to the generation of consciousness, since it . . . attaches . . . to a comparatively quiet lingering, as it were, of the cathexis.

(S.E., pp. 342-3)

The other two issues are the nature of the ego and the neurological laws governing the course taken by a quantity. We will turn soon to the nature of the ego in detail, but here will pursue its formation via the determinants of facilitation.

The crucial importance of the distinction between current in flow and cathexis lies in its relationship to the primary and secondary processes. It will be recalled that 'the principle of inertia finds expression in the hypothesis of a *current*' and that:

A single neurone is thus a model of the whole nervous system with its dichotomy of structure, the axis-cylinder being the organ of discharge. The secondary function [of the nervous system], however, which calls for the accumulation of $Q\dot{\eta}$ [p. 297], is made possible by the assumption of resistances which oppose discharge; and the structure of neurones makes it probable that the resistances are all to be located in the *contacts* [between one neurone and another], which in this way assume the value of *barriers*.

(S.E., p. 298)

But now (p. 368) we are faced with the paradox that the nervous system must be able to be highly cathected, without there being much current in flow.

If we want to reconcile the two, we arrive at the hypothesis of what is, as it were, a *bound state* in the neurone. . . .

(S.E., p. 368)

The suggestion is that when synaptic resistance is not lowered, i.e. when quantity is *not* absorbed by synapses to lower their resistance and produce facilitation, it is stored as cathexis in neurons, i.e. 'bound'. The question remains as to the conditions that determine whether cathexes become 'bound' in neurons and when, on the other hand, cathexes lead to a lowering of synaptic resistance, i.e. to facilitation. And a further question arises: can cathexes be other than bound, i.e. shifting? Freud certainly mentions shifts in cathexes, e.g.:

The struggle between the established facilitations and the changing cathexes is characteristic of the secondary process of reproductive thought, in contrast to the primary sequence of association.

(S.E., p. 329)

Nor is there any question that Freud considers that increased cathexis leads to facilitation, e.g.:

Once again, cathexis is here shown to be equivalent, as regards the passage of $Q\dot{\eta}$, to facilitation [cf. pp. 300–1].

(S.E., p. 319)

There are thus, unquestionably, two sets of conditions apposed. Each becomes clearly detailed: (1) Under circumstances where an increase in cathexis is found on both sides of a contact-barrier, cathexis provides a bias towards an increase in synaptic quantity, i.e. to lowering the threshold (precathexis) for facilitation. This condition which Freud calls the Law of Association by Simultaneity leads to the passage of quantity (conduction of nerve impulses, transmission of excitation) to another location in the nervous system which is in its turn, therefore, cathected. Cathexis has by this route been shifted. (2) The other condition occurs when facilitation is meagre and it is in this condition that cathexis is bound in neurons. The bound condition becomes especially manifest when, as we shall see (p. 73), neurons collateral to the main paths of facilitation become the repository of excitation.

Such lateral or side cathexes tend to bias against, i.e. 'oppose' facilitation by 'draining' off excitation from the main pathways.

Among other things, whether binding or facilitation occurs depends on whether in adjoining neurons excitation builds up simultaneously. When simultaneity is present, a temporary facilitation of the synapses results, while the synapses of other branches of the same neurons would remain unfacilitated because the neighbours with which *these* synapses make contact are relatively unexcited.

It remains to be seen in what else facilitation consists. A first idea might be: in the absorption of $Q\dot\eta$ by the contact-barriers: . . . it is not necessarily the case that the facilitation which remains after a passage of $Q\dot\eta$ is as great as it had to be during the passage. [See p. 316.] Possibly only a quotient of it is left as a *permanent facilitation.*

(S.E., pp. 301–2)

Thus the distinction between binding and facilitation is seen to depend upon where in a neuron energy is utilized. Just as cathexis is thought of as quantity filling the nerve cell, facilitation is suggested to be quantity 'absorbed' by the synapse.

Again we ask, how do Freud's proposals regarding cathexis as presented in the *Project* hold up against today's neurophysiology? With regard to research very little has been directly accomplished. Except for work by Adey, Kado, Didio and Schindler (1963), no one has attempted to distinguish impedance (cathexis) from resistance (the inverse of facilitation) in neuronal tissue and Adey's work was limited to recording from neuronal aggregates rather than from neural units. Despite this, it now appears that Freud's theory is by no means dead, however. Only recently the Law of Association by Simultaneity was seriously revived by Gunther Stent (1973) under the guise of Hebb's postulate because Hebb (in 1949) made a proposal identical to, but independent of, Freud's (which was of course not published until the early fifties). Stent has ingeniously proposed that the Law of Association by Simultaneity can account for the variety of results obtained when neural unit recordings are made in visual cortex after bilateral and unilateral sensory deprivation experiments. Such experiments show that unilateral deprivation leads to a taking over of the unit by inner-vation from the undeprived eye while bilateral deprivation leads to a more balanced deficit that can, under proper circumstances, be more readily restored to normal.

To recapitulate, Freud's model has often been alleged to be a hydro-dynamic one. More correctly it is an energic model. But still more precisely, the conception is based on the electrical concomitants of neural activity which had come to be seriously investigated in the last decades of the 19th century. Impulse transmission (action currents) becomes *current* in flow. Synapses, contact barriers, interpose *resistance* to the flow of current. What remains is *voltage*, and the capacitance of neurons to store potential excitation. Cathexis refers to this third term in Freud's neural version of Ohm's Law. Freud was thus *not* using analogy and metaphor but talking *fact*. He does not suggest that water is running around in the head but rather that electricity is there – there had as yet, of course, been no universally recognized demonstrations of the electroencephalogram although Caton had already provided the first such evidence (1875). This, it seems, is the aim of the *Project*, true to the Helmholtzian tradition in which Freud was steeped: to base a quantitative psychology on physical principles, on an Ohm's Law of neural function.

PHI AND PSI SYSTEMS AND THE MEMORY TRACE

To return to the delineation of the model. The initial problem faced by Freud, the basic problem, is to achieve a neural mechanism that, while it remains receptive and capable of discharge, still maintains the ability to delay and retain excitation.

As those who have tried to simulate neural networks have found out, design of a system with this dual characteristic is beset with difficulties. If the receptive aspects of the system are emphasized, the behaviour of the net is continually modified – i.e. the system is stimulus bound – and it retains little. If, on the other hand, the retentive property is over-emphasized, 'one trial learning' with incapacity for subsequent modification characterizes the behaviour of the system (e.g. Peter Milner, 1957).

The *Project*, therefore, suggests that, in the well-developed organism, these functions are split among two major types of systems. On the one hand are the systems of neurons (ϕ) which by virtue of contact with the environment are primarily responsible for reception and motor discharge; on the other are those systems (ψ) in contact with endogenous excitation which are for the most part given over to retention. This makes sense provided the ϕ systems are selectively made 'permeable' – i.e. their synapses are so thoroughly and generally facilitated that excitation could not be bound. But let the *Project* speak for itself:

It would seem, therefore, that neurones must be both influenced and also unaltered, unprejudiced. We cannot off-hand imagine an apparatus capable

66

of such complicated functioning; the situation is accordingly saved by attributing the characteristic of being permanently influenced by excitation to one class of neurones, and, on the other hand, the unalterability – the characteristic of being fresh for new excitations – to another class. Thus has arisen the current distinction between 'perceptual cells' and 'mnemic cells' – a distinction, however, which fits into no other context and cannot itself appeal to anything in its support.

The theory of contact-barriers, if it adopts this solution, can express it in the following terms. There are two classes of neurones: [1] those which allow $Q\dot{\eta}$ to pass through as though they had no contact-barriers and which, accordingly, after each passage of excitation are in the same state as before, and (2) those whose contact-barriers make themselves felt, so that they only allow $Q\dot{\eta}$ to pass through with difficulty or partially. The latter class may, after each excitation, be in a different state from before and they thus afford a *possibility of representing memory*.

Thus there are *permeable* neurones (offering no resistance and retaining nothing), which serve for perception, and *impermeable* ones (loaded with resistance, and holding back $Q\dot{\eta}$), which are the vehicles of memory and so probably of psychical processes in general. Henceforward I shall call the former system of neurones ϕ and the latter ψ.

(S.E., pp. 299–300)

Again the *Project* anticipates recent neurophysiological inquiries by more than half a century. As noted in Chapter 1, the primary brain – the primitive nuclear masses embedded in the cerebrum, especially the mesencephalic reticular, diencephalic and limbic formations – have been known to serve as the 'head ganglia of the autonomic nervous system' (Sherrington) and to be especially sensitive to a variety of hormones such as adrenergic neurochemicals. But more recently some of these same formations have been critically implicated in human memory (Adams, 1969; Milner and Penfield, 1955; Pribram, 1971). Again, of course, Freud's proposal did not arise in a vacuum. The conjectures of Broca (1878), the work of Sechenov (1863) and of Bechterev's laboratory (1899) and the locally performed experiments of Karplus and Kreidl (1909) were of course well known in Viennese neurological circles.

The distinction Freud draws is thus in many respects similar to that current today between the sense modality specific projection systems and the non-specific, more diffusely organized core systems of the cephalic portion of the neuraxis. The classical sensory-motor projection systems, with their rapid topologically organized conduction paths of long fibre tracts interspersed with few synapses, fulfil the requirements of Freud's ϕ system. The non-specific systems, on the other hand, are made up of many branching neurons, usually shorter than those of the projection systems. They receive stimulation from the external world only through collaterals from the projection systems. Propagation of excitation takes place only under certain, yet to be determined, circumstances in the non-specific systems. The work of Gloor (1955), for instance, has demonstrated that an electrical stimulus in one location will increase the excitation in the dendritic layer of an adjacent structure, but that this increase in graded dendritic potentials fails to be transmitted immediately as impulsive discharge in the tract that leads from this structure. So, the conception – oversimplified though it is – that the central nervous system can be conceived as composed of two types of neural systems is at least as tenable today as it was at the turn of the century.

For Freud the ψ system is the really interesting one. Here several branches of each neuron come in contact with those of others. Here, therefore, *selective* facilitation can take place – and this selective facilitation is the basis of the memory trace.

Glover (1947) has made a cogent case that the basic structural concept of psychoanalysis is a memory trace. We agree and would point out that it proves helpful in making this clear to develop concepts regarding the neural substrate of such memory traces.

A main characteristic of nervous tissue is memory: that is, quite generally, a capacity for being permanently altered by single occurrences – which offers such a striking contrast to the behaviour of a material that permits the passage of a wave-movement and thereafter returns to its former condition. A psychological theory deserving any consideration must furnish an explanation of 'memory'.

(S.E., p. 299)

The needed psychological theory was proposed in neurological terms:

All psych[*olog*]ical *acquisition* would in that case consist in the organization of the ψ system through partial and locally determined lifting of the resistance in the contact-barriers [*italics ours*]. . . .

(S.E., p. 302)

And again:

Memory is represented by the facilitations existing between the ψ neurones.

(S.E., p. 300)

The *Project* thus adopts the simple notion, still commonly held (e.g. Gerard, 1949, 1950, 1960; Eccles, 1964), that repeated transmission of excitation lowers synaptic resistance:

Facilitation depends on the $Q\dot\eta$ which passes through the neurone in the excitatory process and on the number of repetitions of the process.

(S.E., p. 300)

When synaptic resistance is lowered, nerve impulse transmission is facilitated, and pathways (*Bahnung*) are grooved in the nervous system. Memory is, according to this hypothesis, the facilitation of nerve impulse transmission paths and the effect of an experience is proportional to 'magnitude and frequency' of its occurrence. Yet the relationship is not necessarily a direct one.

. . . it is also impossible to tell . . . whether the passage of $Q:3\dot\eta$ once is equivalent to the passage of one $Q\dot\eta$ 3 times. All this remains to be considered in the light of . . . applications of the theory to the psych[*olog*]ical facts.

(S.E., p. 302)

MEMORY AND MOTIVE

What are some of the psychological facts? As we have seen, of critical importance to the model is the neurological fact (p. 65) that every neuron must in general be assumed to have several paths of connections with other neurons, i.e. several contact barriers. This fact allows selective facilitation to occur, so that flow of nerve impulses becomes directional. The psychological conditions under which selective facilitation is favoured become clear when the fact of directionality is recognized as the motive process that guides behaviour:

If we were to suppose that all the ψ contact-barriers were equally well facilitated, or (what is the same thing) offered equal resistance, the characteristics of memory would evidently not emerge. For, in relation to the passage of an excitation, memory is evidently one of the powers which determine and direct its pathway, and, if facilitation were everywhere equal, it would not be possible to see why one pathway should be preferred. We can therefore say still more correctly that *memory is represented by the differences in the facilitations between the ψ neurones.*

(S.E., p. 300)

It now becomes quite clear that the state of facilitation of one contact-barrier must be independent of that of all the other contact-barriers of the same ψ neurone, otherwise there would once again be no preference and thus no *motive* [*italics ours*].

(S.E., p. 301)

From this passage one realizes the identity which the early metapsychology draws between the memory trace and the structure of the motive process. Note that facilitation, because of its selectivity, *also* biases, i.e. directs, the organism's behaviour and thus *is* the motive for that behaviour, one plan or programme being preferred to another. And recall also in this connection (Ch. 1) the close relation between drive and the memory trace – that each memory trace is, in the *Project*, at the least doubly determined: both endogenous and exogenous excitations contribute to the formation of *each* facilitation. Because of its close connection to endogenous excitation the ψ system has the office of relating these to the exigencies of life – i.e. to excitations derived from the external world through collaterals from the ϕ system.

This relationship between memory and drive is summarized succinctly by Rapaport:

... the experience is deposited in the memory systems in a manner influenced by its relation to other deposited material. Instinctual impulses originating in the organism become active in the Unconscious, *and use memories for their representation and expression.*

(Rapaport, 1950a, pp. 158–9)

Finally:

. . . selective forces of instinctual origin and processes of habituation are interlaced in memory function, producing the magnificent and well-nigh impenetrable complexity of men's memory.

(ibid., p. 137)

Both memory and motive are ψ processes based on selective facilitation. To paraphrase this argument succinctly, memories are the retrospective aspects of the facilitations; motives the prospective aspects (see Pribram, 1962). In retrospect, facilitations result from and thus reflect the experiences of the organism; prospectively they are feedforward programmes that run themselves off to completion thus guiding motivating behaviour. We must recall in this respect that the *Project* was written at a time when Freud still believed that the verbal reports of his patients reflected accurately the actual occurrences they had experienced in childhood. When it dawned on him that he was making a serious mistake, Freud modified the emphasis in the model (a change that can be found fully developed in Chapter 7 of *The Interpretation of Dreams* and subsequently) consistent with the new findings that experience can be distorted by the subsequent development of the drive system at puberty. These modifications took the form, foreshadowed in the *Project* (p. 316), of an increased abstraction and autonomy of that part of ψ – the 'nuclear neurones', the 'nucleus of ψ', a 'sympathetic ganglion' – which receives, in the main, the excitations of endogenous origin – the part which is in later writings to become the id.

None the less, the earlier model, the one which concerns us here, was not completely abandoned. Id functions were not divested of their associations with environmental exigencies. Rather, as already pointed out in Ch. 1, the part of ψ concerned mainly with these early and intimate relationships with the environment were also abstracted and given greater autonomy in the form of a structured Superego.

So, there continues to be considerable merit to a further exploration of the original model as detailed in the *Project*. The linkage of motive and memory in the structure of the wish *is* one of the fundamental contributions of psychoanalysis. To paraphrase Rapaport (1950a), the experimental study of memory received contributions from three major currents: Ebbinghaus's (1885) work on rote learning; the *Gestalt* emphasis on the lawful organization of the content of remembering; and the psychoanalytic view that memory is so intricately interwoven with motive. The model of a memory-motive structure based on the development of selective facilitations between branching neurons presented in the *Project* provides a mechanism which parallels the clinical psychoanalytic contribution. Thus, tests can now be made both at the neurological and the behavioural level outside the analytic situation. Neurologically changes of facilitation resulting from specific experience have already been demonstrated with respect to development, i.e. during sensitive periods critical to the establishing of specific behaviours such as visual pattern discrimination (see e.g. review by Riesen, 1970). What remains to be shown is the extent to which such changes occur in the adult. At a behavioural level, a network of selective facilitations is akin to a computer programme – almost all current experimentation in cognitive psychology is therefore cogent (Neisser, 1967; Reitman, 1965; Broadbent, 1973).

DEFENCE THROUGH DELAY OF DISCHARGE

The distinction between a primary function of immediate discharge of neural excitation and a secondary, equilibratory, function is, as we have seen, a fundamental one in the *Project*. From this distinction the differentiation between primary and secondary processes is developed. We recall that the secondary process results from the fact that when the system receives endogenous stimuli from the somatic element that these 'only cease subject to particular conditions, which must be realized in the external world' (p. 297). It is the action undertaken under these 'particular conditions' that are called 'specific actions':

It [*the ψ system*] must put up with [maintaining] a store of $Q\dot\eta$ sufficient to meet the demand for a specific action . . . the manner in which it does this shows that the same trend persists, modified . . . to keep the $Q\dot\eta$ as low as possible and to guard against any increase of it – that is, to keep it constant.

(S.E., p. 297)

How, then, are specific actions achieved? The model of ψ – the memory-motive neural mechanism – so far presented would lead one to believe that organisms exist in a continual 'wishful' state of neural excitation. As already noted, such an activated state may, at any moment, result either in impulsive motor or, through key neurons, in endogenous endocrine discharge. So by way of inappropriate behaviour with its unpleasant social consequences, or by way of the biochemical 'unpleasure' positive feedback loop, the organism is plunged into a cycle of ever-augmenting tension, or as we today would put it, an elevation of set point leading to increasing activation (Ch. 1). But organisms do not appear to exist in this precarious state. Obviously the nervous system is so constructed that any accruing spiral of increasing tension is defended against (pp. 323-4). What is the neurological nature of these defences which, in their totality, lead to the formation of a structure called the 'ego'?

. . . an organization has been formed in ψ whose presence interferes with passages [of quantity]. . . . This organization is called the '*ego*'.

(S.E., p. 323)

The way in which this organization is constructed is presented in great detail (diagram included):

A $Q\dot\eta$ which breaks into a neurone from anywhere will proceed in the direction of the contact-barrier with the largest facilitation and will set up a current in that direction. To put this more accurately: the $Q\dot\eta$ current will divide up in the direction of the various contact-barriers in inverse ratio to their resistance; and, in that case, where a contact-barrier is impinged upon by a quotient which is inferior to its [the contact-barrier's] resistance, nothing will in practice pass through there. This relation may easily turn out differently in the case of each $Q\dot\eta$ in the neurone, for quotients may then arise which are superior to the threshold at other contact-barriers as well. Thus the course taken is dependent on $Q\dot\eta$ and the relation of the facilitations. We have, however, come to know the third powerful factor [p. 319]. If an adjoining neurone is simultaneously cathected, this acts like a temporary facilitation of the contact-barrier lying between the two, and modifies the course [of the current], which would otherwise have been directed towards the one facilitated contact-barrier. A *side-cathexis* thus acts as *an inhibition of the course of* $Q\dot{\eta}$. Let us picture the ego as a network of cathected neurones well facilitated in relation to one another [*but inhibitory with respect to the memory-motive structure because they branch away from its major pathways*] thus: [see Fig. 3]. If we suppose that a $Q\dot{\eta}$ enters a neurone *a* from outside (ϕ),

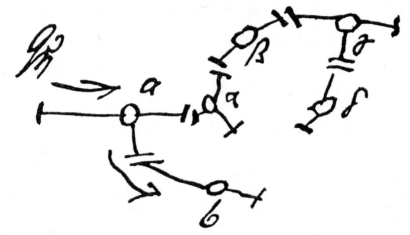

Fig. 3. Freud's diagram of the manner in which connections are established in the system.

then, if it were uninfluenced, it would pass to neurone *b*; but it is so much influenced by the side-cathexis *a–a* that it gives off only a quotient to *b* and may even perhaps not reach *b* at all. Therefore, if an ego [*the side cathexes*] exists, it must *inhibit* psychical primary processes.

Inhibition of this kind is, however, a decided advantage to ψ. Let us suppose that *a* is a hostile mnemic image and *b* a key neurone to unpleasure [p. 320]. Then, if *a* is awakened, primarily unpleasure would be released, which would perhaps be pointless and is so in any case [if released] to its full amount. With an inhibitory action from *a*, the release of unpleasure will turn out very slight and the nervous system will be spared the development and discharge of Q without any other damage. It is easy now to imagine how, with the help of a mechanism which draws the ego's *attention* [*see Ch. 3*] to the imminent fresh cathexis of the hostile mnemic image, the ego can succeed in inhibiting the passage [of quantity] from a mnemic image to a release of unpleasure by a copious side-cathexis which can be strengthened according to need. Indeed, if we suppose that the original $Q\dot{\eta}$ release of unpleasure is taken up [*in this way*] by the [*side cathexis of the*] ego itself, we shall have in it itself the source of the expenditure which is required by the inhibiting side-cathexis from the ego. In that case, the stronger the unpleasure, the stronger will be the primary defence.

(S.E., pp. 323–4)

A definition of 'primary defence' is repeatedly given as: 'non-cathexis owing to the threat of unpleasure' (p. 370). This is consequent on the operation of a 'biological rule', by which the memory traces that compose the primary defence have achieved a higher threshold (today we would say by hyperpolarization, i.e. by inhibition). In the terms of the *Project* the facilitations leading to the key neurons have become non-cathected with respect to the rest of the ψ apparatus.

Once the primary defence is assumed, its continuing operation will, as we will shortly see, lead to the construction of the ego, the normal delay and inhibiting processes. But the operation of the neural process that initially draws cathexes away from the pathways that would lead to discharge and so produce unpleasure must constitute a biological given – an inherent, inherited 'consequence of the original trend of the nervous system'. The mechanism involved is not all that easy to determine, however:

How *primary defence*, non-cathexis owing to a threat of unpleasure, is to be represented mechanically – this, I confess, I am unable to say.

(S.E., p. 370)

Actually, considerable understanding of mechanism is provided. One can make out three steps in the development of the delay process that constitutes defence as this is discussed in various places in the *Project*. The first, initial step is one of *reflex* defence. This is presumably a built-in high threshold circuit, a 'biological rule' (p. 371) which probably operates by shunting discharge by way of facilitations to the muscular system (S.E., pp. 296-7). This is followed, as we have seen, by the development of lateral cathexes co-extensive with the memory-motive structures of the wish.

It seems to us, therefore, that the pessimistic passage where Freud disclaims ability to offer an answer must be taken with a grain of salt. True, the determinants of the exact balance between facilitation and inhibition escape him, but this is hardly a fatal flaw in the model, which perhaps more simply stated, proposes that the pathways towards motor discharge have innately lower thresholds than those to neuro-secretory neurons. Since the primary motor mechanism is located in ϕ, one wonders why Freud did not use here the argument he so ingeniously uses to separate ϕ from ψ (Ch. 1): primary motor pathways,

74

just as primary sensory, are characterized by a paucity of synapses and thus would tend to show low resistances, i.e. in contrast to the multisynaptic endogenous circuits, the motor pathways would become easily facilitated.

Finally, the normal secondary ψ processes of delay become established. These make possible a continuing comparison between the excitations orginating in the memory structures of ψ and those initiated in ϕ. The results of these comparisons between experienced wish and the perception of reality lead, by a process of neural inhibition – i.e. of delaying premature discharge, to the ordered growth of the network of neurons in ψ which when cathected become the will. This normal operation leading to specific action is called, as we have seen, the secondary process; when it fails, because, for some reason, the balance between facilitation and inhibition is tipped against the latter, more *primary* wishful processes, invoking primary and even *reflex* defence, are brought into operation.

So then: if there is inhibition by a cathected ego, the indications of [*cortical*] discharge become quite generally *indications of reality*, which ψ learns, biologically, to make use of. If, when an *indication of reality* of this kind emerges, the ego is in a state of wishful tension, it will allow discharge towards the specific action to follow [p. 318]. If an increase of unpleasure coincides with the *indication of reality*, then ψ will, by means of a side-cathexis of suitable magnitude, institute a defence of normal magnitude at the point indicated. If neither of these is the case, the cathexis will be allowed to proceed unhindered according to the circumstances of the facilitations. Wishful cathexis to the point of hallucination [and] complete generation of unpleasure which involves a complete expenditure of defence are described by us as *psychical primary processes*; by contrast, those processes which are only made possible by a good cathexis of the ego, and which represent a moderation of the foregoing, are described as *psychical secondary processes*. It will be seen that the necessary precondition of the latter is a correct employment of the *indications of reality*, which is only possible when there is inhibition by the ego.

(S.E., pp. 326–7)

Gill (1963) has suggested that there must be a *hierarchy of defences* running from the primary to the secondary process pole. Here in this early work, the *Project*, we find the clear description of primary process, excessive or pathological defence and of secondary process, moderated defence. Freud discusses these levels of defence in Part II of the *Project*, which is titled 'Psychopathology' (pp. 351–2). We will take these up in greater detail in Chapter 5 in our discussion of that part of the *Project*.

THE EGO AS EXECUTIVE

This opposition of primary and secondary processes – of facilitatory memory-motive wish and inhibitory ego defence structures – which allows 'specific actions' to occur calls to mind a current issue in cognitive psychology. The problem is this: if in fact behaviour is directed by a variety of memory-motive structures, programmes and plans, how is a decision achieved as to which of these structures is to guide behaviour at any specified moment? Neisser reviews this contemporary problem as follows:

Most psychological theories are 'conventional' in this respect. The notion of a separate processor, or *executive*, is rejected not only by classical association theory but by behaviorism, by the 'trace theory' of Rock and Ceraso (1964), and by Gestalt psychology (except for a few cryptic passages in Koffka, 1935). It is also missing from Freud's notion of 'primary-process thinking'. Freud was quick to postulate executive processes of many kinds as well (e.g., the ego, . . .) but he was usually more interested in what they suppressed than in what they produced.

A 'conventional' theorist can deal with executive phenomena in two ways. First, he can classify them as 'higher mental processes' and thus as outside his area of interest. Second, he can treat them directly, but this means that he must *reduce* them to conventional cases. He is obliged to argue that appearances are deceptive: what seems like an executive process is really the simple resultant of existing response strengths, and what seems like fresh and adaptive behavior is only the reappearance of previous elements. My own view is quite different. Appearances are indeed deceptive in many experiments, but they deceive at least as often in studies of 'rote learning' as in work on thinking. What seems to be simple associative revival of earlier responses may actually be a complex process of search and construction; a subject instructed to memorize syllables by rote tends instead to construct complex rhythmic and semantic patterns which incorporate them. In this sense remembering is always a form of problem-solving, and therefore a higher mental process. That is why it is treated as one in this book. (A similar treatment appears in Miller, Galanter and Pribram, 1960, Ch. 10.)

(Neisser, 1967, p. 294)

Now let us hear out the *Project* once more on this topic:

. . . by contrast [*to primary processes*], those processes which are only made possible by a good cathexis of the ego, and which represent a moderation of the foregoing [*primary processes*], are described as *psychical secondary processes*.

(S.E., p. 327)

And to remind us that wish, the memory-motive structure, is a primary process which becomes modulated by an inhibitory ego to produce the secondary process:

We have brought forward the hypothesis that, during the process of wishing, inhibition by the ego brings about a moderated cathexis of the object wished-for, which allows it to be cognized as not real; . . .

(S.E., p. 327)

Freud, in proceeding with the analysis of this process, goes further. He distinguishes clearly in his model between an executive 'nucleus of the ego' and 'changing cathexes'. In the following quotation, bear in mind that Freud cautions us in the *Project* to interpret 'neurone *a*' and 'neurone *b*' as representations of systems of neurons '*a*' and '*b*'.

A way is now found, however, of completing the similarity [*between wish and percept – see Ch. 3*] into an identity. The perceptual complex, if it is compared with other perceptual complexes, can be dissected into a component portion, neurone *a*, which on the whole remains the same, and a second component portion, neurone *b*, which for the most part varies. Language will later apply the term *judgement* [*see Ch. 3*] to this dissection and will discover the re-semblance which in fact exists between the nucleus of the ego and the constant perceptual component [on the one hand] and between the changing cathexes [*due to activation of the memory-motive structure of the wish*] in the pallium [pp. 315 and 323] and the inconstant component [on the other]; it [language] will call neurone *a* the thing [*or object*] and neurone *b* its activity or attribute – in short, its *predicate*.

(S.E., p. 328)

There is much more on this topic which is the concern of Chapters 3 and 4, which detail the way in which the *Project* deals with remembering (recognizing) and thinking as forms of problem solving. But before proceeding to these chapters, it is important to understand why the problem of an executive ego has been swept under the rug, as it were, in much of contemporary cognitive psychology and what the current neuropsychological facts are regarding executive function in the brain. Neisser deals with this issue explicitly:

It is important to understand why the hypothesis of a separate executive process has always been rejected by the 'conventional' theories. The most commonly cited ground is the law of parsimony, 'Occam's Razor': con-structs should not be elaborated more than is necessary. But this razor has two edges; Granit has remarked that '. . . the biologist's attitude should be humbler. His duty is to admit that he does not know nature well enough to understand her requirements of "necessities". That is why he experiments' (1955, p. 37).

In any case, the law of parsimony would hardly explain the very un-parsimonious hypotheses erected by stimulus-response theorists to explain away what seem to be executive processes. Their real motive is a more serious one. They are afraid that a separate executive would return psychology to the soul, the will, and the *homunculus*; it would be equivalent to explaining behavior in terms of a 'little man in the head'. Such explanations seem to lead only to an infinite regress, which must bar further research and frustrate theory. If the actions of the executive account for behavior, what accounts for those actions in turn? Does the ego have an ego?

It now seems possible that there is an escape from the regress that formerly seemed infinite. As recently as a generation ago, processes of control had to be thought of as *homunculi*, because man was the only known model of an executive agent. Today, the stored-program computer has provided us with an alternative possibility, in the form of the *executive routine*. This is a concept which may be of considerable use to psychology.

Most computer programs consist of largely independent parts, or 'subroutines'. In complex sequential programs, the order in which the subroutines are applied will vary from one occasion to the next. . . . Common practice is to make all subroutines end by transferring control to [another program known as] the executive, which then decides what to do next in each case. One might well say that the executive 'uses' the other routines, which are 'subordinate' to it. Some programs may even have a hier-archical structure, in which routines at one level can call those which are 'lower' and are themselves called by others which are 'higher'. However, the regress of control is not infinite: there is a 'highest', or executive routine which is not used by anything else.

Note that the executive is in no sense a *programmulus*, or miniature of the entire program. It does not carry out the tests or the searches or the constructions which are the task of the subroutines, and it does not include the stored information which the subroutines use. Indeed, the executive may take only a small fraction of the computing time and space allotted to the program as a whole, and it need not contain any very sophisticated processes.

(Neisser, 1967, pp. 294–6)

Compare these statements by Neisser working in the domain of cognitive behaviour theory with those by Pribram (1967a) working in brain physiology:

. . . this corticofugal model of the functions of the so-called association systems relieves us of the problem of infinite regress – an association area homunculus who synthesizes and abstracts from inputs, only to pass on these abstractions to a still higher homunculus, perhaps the one who makes decisions.

The problem of the homunculus is, of course, an extremely interesting one. Former ways of looking at the input-output relationships of the brain have come up against the problem of an infinite regression (implicit or explicit) of little men inside little men – homunculi associating sensations, abstracting from these associations and passing these abstractions on to the motor systems for action. Somewhere along the line of regress awareness comes in, perhaps yet another anatomically separable system; and then there is awareness of awareness. According to the model presented here, there is no need for such infinite regress. Important functions such as perception and decision are going on within the primary sensory and motor projection systems. Other brain regions such as the posterior sensory-specific associated systems and the frontolimbic systems exert their effects by altering the functional organization of the primary systems. Thus these systems are *not* 'association' systems; they simply alter the configurations of input-output relationships processed by the classical systems. In computer language the associated systems function by supplying *subroutines* in a hierarchy of programs, subroutines contained within and not superimposed above the more fundamental processes. In this fashion the infinite abstractive regress is avoided. One could argue that it is replaced by a downward regress of sub- and subsubroutines; to me this type of regress is the more under-standable and manipulatable. The posterior association cortex is conceived simply to program, to structure, an input channel, perhaps through action on recurrent inhibitory collaterals within the channel. The effect of such action is to alter the speed of recovery of neurons in the channel once they are excited by inputs. And by means of the operation of such a simple device, information processing, sampling of the environment, and selective attention 'automatically' follow.

Another advantage of the model is that the signal itself is not altered; the invariant properties of a signal are unaffected (unless channel capacity is over-reached). It is only the channel itself – the channel within which the signal is transmitted – which is altered. Thus, the same signal carries more or less information, depending on the 'width' of the channel. I am tempted to extrapolate and say that the signal carries different meanings depending on the particular structure or organization of the redundancy of the channel.

(Pribram, 1967a, pp. 109–11)

Note here the similarity to the statements in the *Project* quoted above regarding an unaltered 'thing' component and a varying 'predicate' component of the process.

Elsewhere, Pribram (Pribram, Ahumada, Hartog and Roos, 1964; Pribram and Luria, 1973, Ch. 14) has detailed the currently available neurological evidence for the operation of this executive process. It differs from Freud's chiefly in the proposal that delay in the execution of any particular behaviour (motor discharge in the terms of the *Project*) is accomplished by a complete interruption of one memory-motive process in favour of another (Miller, Galanter and Pribram, 1960) rather than by selectively 'delaying' and modifying wishful

79

cathexes. But just as in the *Project*, these executive functions are classed as 'willed', 'intentional' or 'voluntary' in control theory and neurology since they depend on feedforward rather than feedback mechanisms (McFarland, 1971; Miller, Galanter and Pribram, 1960; Pribram, 1971). It is interesting that the neural system responsible for this interruption is labelled 'inhibitory' by neurophysiologists reporting its effects on reflex behaviour and on electrical brain activity (Skinner and Lindsley in Pribram and Luria, 1973) just as Freud spoke of lateral cathexes as inhibitory. However, this in no way implies that such inhibition takes place by way of lateral or side-cathexes, whose role would be limited to the *development* of memory-motive structures on the basis of the Law of Association by Simultaneity (Stent, 1973). A more plausible explanation is that the system is constituted so that it produces inhibition (hyperpolarization) at the critical terminations (synapses) by way of its neurochemical transmitter. In short, we now conceive of separate excitatory and inhibitory systems of neurons (in mammals at least; invertebrates show excitatory and inhibitory branches on the same neuron) where Freud obtained inhibition by way of establishing sidepaths orthogonal to the facilitating mechanism. Thus Pribram states:

I feel reasonably sure that the dorsolateral frontal cortex, like the limbic formations of the forebrain (including the medial and orbital frontal cortex), are concerned in the inhibition of interference among brain events. With respect to lesions of the frontal cortex, this involvement becomes manifest on the input side as a difficulty in attention, a difficulty in registering novelty so that habituation fails to take place. On the output side, the feedback to actions from their outcomes is impaired and reinforcers become relatively ineffective.

The intact frontal brain tissue must help to accomplish registration and reinforcement by some not too complicated mechanism. What could be its nature? In order to obtain some clue, I turn, as I so often have in the past, to the analogy of those hardware brains, especially computers, that so effectively mimic many of the functions ordinarily carried on by the wetware in our heads (Miller et al., 1960; Pribram et al., 1964; Pribram, 1971). Mechanical as well as biological thinking machines continually face the simultaneous demands of a variety of inputs and outcomes. These could easily interfere with one another and with any of the central operations being carried on at the moment by the computer. To prevent this, some noticing order must govern the acceptance of first this, then that, product of the input-output devices. In its simplest form, each of these devices is fitted with a marker or flag, which decrees that while busy with its productions, the computer temporarily shuts off the paths to and from other devices. In more complicated forms, only part of the computer may be thus preempted, or a program can be used to regulate the flow of information. Simple flexible noticing order programs have been used for years for this purpose; more recently these have burgeoned into full scale executive routines that effect the timesharing of large multiple user machines.

(Pribram and Luria, 1973, pp. 306–8)

The reader is referred to the original for the experimental details upon which the model is based. Here we are concerned in keeping what is effective and disposing of what needs to be discarded in the early conceptualizations found in the *Project*. To us it seems that there the problems are set forth admirably. The neurophysiological solution presented by Freud can, however, be modified in the light of current knowledge. Our reading of the *Project* makes it clear that Freud describes separate neurological memory-motive (facilitatory) and ego (inhibitory) structures, structures we would today call cognitive structures and details for us their separate and interactive functions. Further, both in the *Project* and in contemporary neurophysiology the ego's executive processes operate primarily by way of inhibitory influences on a facilitatory structure by a feedforward directive, willed, intentional and voluntary (but not necessarily 'conscious' – see Ch. 3) process. In the *Project* these executive processes have been shown to slowly defend against the accruing excitation which results when the key secretory neurons are stimulated to initiate the 'generation of unpleasure'.

There is, therefore, a remaining puzzle. An apparatus has been portrayed, a model described, which, by means of an ego, an executive, operating on an arrangement of memory-motive structures, makes possible willed actions specific to the exigencies of the internal and external environment. But as we have already seen (p. 74), there is some difficulty in getting this model under way – the step from reflex to primary defence can only be explained by invoking 'a biological rule'. And whenever the apparatus is exposed to larger amounts of excitation, ego processes, as described so far, are easily overwhelmed. This is not the actual condition in the normal individual, of course. What constitutes the mechanism which provides the cement that allows ego processes to develop? Just when does the ego, through its inhibitory mechanism, prevent inappropriate peremptory discharge? Psycho-analytic formulations have often been accused of inadequacy with respect to a viable learning theory. Yet an important part of the answer to the question of the structure of the ego is given in the *Project* in terms of a discussion of a learning theory: the development of the process of satisfaction.

SATISFACTION AND THE DEVELOPMENT OF THE EGO

The *Project* handles 'learning' by way of a mechanism of satisfaction, a process we today would describe as reinforcing. When the normal defence mechanism is operating, the organism can experience satisfactions. The process by which satisfactions are accomplished emphasizes once more the fact that the psychoanalytic metapsychology is truly a neuropsychology. Again the course of events that meshes endogenous stimulation with experiences of caretaking persons is described, but in this instance emphasis is on the manner in which pain and unpleasure are brought to an end – i.e. the way in which pleasure, the relief of tension, occurs.

When the helpful person has performed the work of the specific action in the external world for the helpless one, the latter is in a position, by means of reflex contrivances, immediately to carry out in the interior of his body the activity necessary for removing the endogenous stimulus. The total event then constitutes an *experience of satisfaction*, which has the most radical results on the development of the individual's functions.

(S.E., p. 318)

Note here once more that Freud attributes the origins of satisfying experiences to intervention by a caretaking person. Only by such intervention can the memory-motive structures cathected as wishes develop sufficient complexity; only by such intervention can the inhibitory ego become organized. For wishes are the 'residues', i.e. the memory traces, of satisfactory experiences (Ch. 1) and inhibition becomes necessary when, in Freud's own words, 'states of craving', having been through experience altered into 'states of wishing', become further modified into 'states of expecting' (S.E., p. 361) – states that allow reality testing, which is the subject matter taken up in the next chapter. But a preview of the issue as it relates to the development of the ego is in order here:

... three things occur in the ψ system: (1) a lasting discharge is effected and so the urgency which had produced unpleasure in ω is brought to an end; (2) a cathexis of one (or several) of the neurones which correspond to the perception of an object [*see Ch. 3*] occurs in the pallium; and (3) at other points of the pallium information arrives of the discharge of the released reflex movement which follows upon the specific action. A facilitation is then formed between these cathexes and the nuclear neurones.

The information of the reflex discharge comes about because every movement, through its subsidiary results, becomes the occasion for fresh sensory excitations (from the skin and muscles) which give rise to a *motor* (kinaesthetic) *image* [*see Ch. 3*] in ψ.

(S.E., p. 318)

Satisfaction is thus basic to the whole development of the conscious psychological process as detailed in the next chapter. But both as an introduction to Chapter 3 and a summary of this chapter, the following passage serves to highlight the development of executive functions of the ego. This description of the ego, in what Freud calls a 'genetic treatment', is surely one of the first clear statements of what has been called the 'genetic point of view of metapsychology' (Rapaport and Gill, 1959):

Thus we find ourselves quite unexpectedly before the most obscure problem: the origin of the 'ego' – that is, of a complex of neurones which hold fast to their cathexis, a complex, therefore, which is for short periods at a constant level [p. 323]. A genetic treatment will be the most instructive. The ego consists originally of the nuclear neurones, which receive endogenous $Q\dot{\eta}$ through paths of conduction [p. 315] and discharge it along the pathway to internal change [p. 317]. The experience of satisfaction has brought about an association between this nucleus [*producing a wishful image*] and a perceptual image and information of a movement ([information of] the reflex portion of the specific action) [p. 318]. The education and development of this original ego takes place in a repetitive state of [*wishful*] craving, in expectation [p. 361]. It [the ego] learns first that it must not cathect the motor images, so that discharge results, until certain conditions have been fulfilled from the direction of the perception. It learns further that it must not cathect the wishful idea beyond a certain amount since otherwise it would deceive itself in a hallucinatory manner [pp. 325–6]. *If, however, it respects these two barriers and directs its attention to the new perceptions, it has a prospect of attaining the satisfaction it is seeking* [*italics ours*]. It is clear, therefore, that the barriers which prevent the ego from cathecting the wishful image and the motor image beyond a certain amount are the ground for an accumulation of $Q\dot{\eta}$ in the ego, and compel it, perhaps, to transfer its $Q\dot{\eta}$ within certain limits to the neurones accessible to it. . . . Thereafter, the whole cathectic mass is in equilibrium, held on one side by the two barriers against motility and wishing and on the other side by the resistances of the furthest neurones, and towards the interior by the constant pressure [*high threshold*] of the paths of conduction. Inside this ego-structure the cathexis will by no means be everywhere equal; it need only be equal proportionately – that is, in relation to the facilitations [cf. p. 336].

If the level of cathexis in the ego-nucleus rises, the extent of the ego will be able to expand its range; if it [the level] sinks, the ego will narrow concentrically. At a given level and a given extent of the ego there will be nothing to prevent displacement being possible within the area of cathexis.

(S.E., pp. 369–70)

Critical in this passage is the role of attention which 'directs' the ego to 'new perceptions'. Before we can attain a full understanding of the neuropsychological mechanism, the metapsychology, we must have clearly in mind not only the ψ processes of facilitatory memory-motive and inhibitory ego mechanisms, but the conscious processes: imaging the wish; perceiving; judging (comparing wish and percept); motor imaging; reality testing; and the wilful, intentional achievement of specific actions. These ω processes make up the substance of Chapter 3.

[3]

THE THEORY OF
CONSCIOUSNESS

PERCEPTION

In this and the succeeding chapter we come into contact with an ever richer delineation of cognitive theory. In each instance a detailed neurological mechanism is proposed and we thus can critically evaluate not only the conception of the cognitive process *per se*, but its purported neural mechanism in the light of contemporary knowledge. Here we only *initiate* such evaluations to show their feasibility; a more comprehensive treatment could take up many volumes and involve a considerable amount of new research effort.

Thus, we pursue the organization of psychological processes further; our attention is first focused on a subdivision of ψ which becomes the third type of neural system described in the *Project*.

The immediate reason for parcellation of ψ is that a substrate is needed that can handle quality, i.e. (as noted in the introduction) the problem of conscious awareness (*Wahrnehmung*) which includes such sensory qualities as colour and shape, roughness, sweetness and melody.

In that case, however, a place has to be found for the content of consciousness in our quantitative ψ processes. Consciousness gives us what are called *qualities* – sensations which are *different* in a great multiplicity of ways and whose *difference* is distinguished according to its relations with the external world. Within this difference there are series, similarities and so on, but there are in fact no quantities in it.

(S.E., p. 308)

To trace Freud's thinking on this matter we must first retrace and take a look at the quantitative ψ process. Quantity, we recall, is defined in terms of neural excitation, i.e. neurochemical events and their electrical concomitants. How is neural excitation distributed in the ψ system? The *Project* proposes the following sequence of events to occur:

85

... the sensory path of conduction in ϕ is constructed in a peculiar fashion. It ramifies continually and exhibits thicker and thinner paths, which end in numerous terminal points – probably with the following significance: ... the larger quantity in ϕ will be expressed by the fact that it cathects several neurones in ψ instead of a single one. The different cathexes of the ψ neurones may in this case be approximately equal. If [one] $Q\dot{\eta}$ in ϕ gives rise to a cathexis in ψ, then $3(Q\dot{\eta})$ is expressed by a cathexis in $\psi_1 + \psi_2 + \psi_3 \ldots$ By this means the Q is held back from ψ, within certain limits at least. This is very reminiscent of the conditions of *Fechner's* law, which might in this way be localized.

(S.E., p. 314-15)

What then of quality? We have already noted in the Introduction and in Chapter 1, that the *Project* identified the problem of quality with the occurrence of neural periodicities:

Thus we summon up courage to assume that there is a third system of neurones – ω perhaps [we might call it] – which is excited along with perception, but not along with reproduction, and whose states of excitation give rise to the various qualities – are, that is to say, *conscious sensations*.

(S.E., p. 309)

Further,

It would seem as though the characteristic of quality (that is, conscious sensation) comes about only where quantities [*which, as we have seen, imply high resistances and so sluggishness in response*] are so far as possible excluded. It cannot be got rid of entirely, since we must think of the ω neurones too as cathected with $Q\dot{\eta}$ and striving towards discharge.

At this point, however, we are met by what seems to be an immense difficulty. We have seen [p. 300] that permeability depends on the effect of $Q\dot{\eta}$, and the ψ neurones are already impermeable. With still smaller $Q\dot{\eta}$, the ω neurones would have to be still more impermeable. But that is a characteristic that we cannot grant to the vehicles of consciousness. The mutability of their content, the transitoriness of consciousness, the easy linking of qualities simultaneously perceived – all of this tallies only with complete permeability of the ω neurones, together with total *restitutio in integrum* [restoration of their former state]. The ω neurones behave like organs of perception, and in them we could find no place for a memory [p. 299]. Permeability, then, complete facilitation [*is required*], which does not arise from quantity. From where else [can it arise]?

I can see only one way out of the difficulty: a revision of our fundamental hypothesis about the passage of $Q\dot{\eta}$. So far I have regarded it only as the transference of $Q\dot{\eta}$ from one neurone to another. But it must have still another characteristic, of a temporal nature; for the mechanics of the physicists have allowed this temporal characteristic to the other motions of masses in the external world as well. I speak of this as *period* for short. Thus I shall assume that all the resistance of the contact-barriers applies only to the transference of Q, but that the *period* of the neuronal motion is transmitted without inhibition in all directions, as though it were a process of induction.

Here very much remains to be done in the way of physical clarification, for here too the general laws of motion must apply without contradiction. The hypothesis goes further, however, [and assumes] that the ω neurones are incapable of receiving $Q\dot{\eta}$, but that instead they appropriate the *period* of the excitation and that this state of theirs of being affected by period while they are filled with the minimum of $Q\dot{\eta}$ is the fundamental basis of consciousness. The ψ neurones too have their period, of course; but it is without quality or, more correctly, *monotonous*. Deviations from this psychical period that is specific for them come to consciousness as qualities.

(S.E., pp. 309–10)

The *Project* thus solves the problem: something about the periodicity of neural discharge is responsible for consciousness. The transmission of periodicity is not necessarily correlated with that of quantity; in this fashion the neurons of the ω system can be sensitive to changes in periodicity, to patterns, yet become only minimally cathected.

What has modern neurophysiology to say about the possibility that such a mechanism exists (without necessarily referring it to consciousness)?

Some years ago Weiss (1952) performed an interesting experiment. He transplanted a leg of an amblystoma to the chest. Innervated now by thoracic nerves, how would the leg react when the animal tried to swim? Would its muscles contract at the appropriate moment in the sequence of swimming movements or would contraction be haphazard? The leg moved as if it were in its original location. In fact, legs and arms can be interchanged and, when this has been done and a piece of food is placed in front of the beast, it paddles rapidly *away* from the food.

Or interchange a piece of skin from the belly and back of a frog. Now place a little dilute acid on the frog's back. He lifts his leg and scratches his belly.

The results of these experiments cannot be accounted for on the basis of the spatial arrangement of innervation (see Pribram, 1971, p. 261; and Jacobson, 1970, p. 116). Legs react as legs even though innervated by arm nerves. The configuration of a scratch reflex persists even though different nerves are involved after transplantation. The suggestion is that there is some mechanism other than the spatial arrangement of connections by which the nervous system carries out these controls over behaviour. The obvious candidate is some frequency sensitive mechanism.

J. Z. Young and his collaborators (1956a and b) have provided some supporting evidence for such a mechanism. This work has shown (in cats and man) that each muscle group determines the specific fibre diameter size spectrum of its innervation. Fibre diameter is, of course, correlated with size of nerve cell and speed of conduction of impulses. A specific anatomical spectrum is therefore suggestive of a specific distribution of arrivals and departures of nerve impulses – specifically of periodicities.

But there is more. Arrival and departure patterns of nerve impulses would still be highly correlated with local changes of excitation. At first one would therefore assume that nerve impulses and periodicity could not be uncoupled. But we recall that arrivals and departures of nerve impulses occur at synapses; these are characterized by resistances. Recall also that facilitation was stated to be an active process occurring at the synapse. It is here, therefore, that we should look for Freud's periodicity phenomenon. And indeed this is what he himself suggests:

The theory of contact-barriers, if it adopts this solution, can express it in the following terms. There are two classes of neurones: [1] those which allow $Q\dot{\eta}$ to pass through as though they had no contact-barriers and which, accordingly, after each passage of excitation are in the same state as before, and (2) those whose contact-barriers make themselves felt. . . .

(S.E., p. 299)

Thus there are *permeable* neurones (offering no resistance and retaining nothing), which serve for perception, and *impermeable* ones (loaded with resistance, and holding back $Q\dot{\eta}$), which are the vehicles of memory and so probably of psychical processes in general.

(S.E., pp. 299–300)

And what is this property of permeable neurons that allows immutability? Freud considers it a 'material that permits the passage of wave-movement and thereafter returns to its former condition' (S.E., p. 299).

It is necessary here only to recall to attention the interference pattern theory of cortical function proposed by Lashley (1942) and quantified by Beurle (1956), and to point out that this view of things neural is still an actively held one today (Pribram, 1971, Chs. 6–8). Furthermore, this theory has gained substantially in the past few years through translation into the language and data of laboratory neurophysiology by Eccles, Ito and Szentagothai (1967). Eccles shows that wave fronts of interference patterns are indeed set up by the events occurring *at the synapse.* Contemporary neurophysiology, by taking cognizance of the periodicity of neural excitation, is thus coming to conceive a second property of synaptic function. (The first property was facilitation.) In the *Project*, periodicities were not conceived as interference patterns and were presumed to occur only when facilitation is complete. Today, we need make no such assumption and have a better understanding of the two process mechanism of brain function (Pribram, 1971, Chs. 1, 2). Yet there is a striking similarity to the early metapsychology: facilitation, when it is selective, accounts in both models for memory; 'periodicity' (in terms of its reciprocal, spatial and temporal frequency), for perception.

THE CENTRAL 'SENSE ORGANS'

A final word about the phi (ϕ), psi (ψ) and omega (ω) systems. The attributes that account for memory and for perception are not equally distributed throughout the central nervous system. On the basis of anatomical connection some specificities develop:

The quantity of the ϕ excitation is expressed in ψ by complication [*better translated as complexity, as it is on p. 362*], its quality is expressed topographically, since, according to their anatomical relations, the different sense-organs are in communication through ϕ only with particular ψ neurones. But ψ receives cathexis as well from the interior of the body; and it is probable that the ψ neurones should be divided into two groups; the neurones of the *pallium* which are cathected from ϕ [*and contain ω*] and the *nuclear* neurones which are cathected from the endogenous paths of conduction.

(S.E., p. 315)

There were several changes in the relationship between ϕ, ψ and ω over the next years. In the *Project* the operation of ψ was placed between ϕ and ω:

The qualitative characteristic of the stimuli now proceeds **unhindered** through ϕ by way of ψ to ω, where it generates sensation. . . .

(S.E., p. 314)

He had also written:

The filling of ω neurones with $Q\dot{\eta}$ can no doubt only proceed from ψ, since we do not wish to admit any direct link between this third system and ϕ.

(S.E., p. 311)

But in a letter to Fliess on 1st January 1896 he put ω between ϕ and ψ:

In my new scheme I insert these perceptual neurones (ω) between the ϕ-neurones and the ψ-neurones; so that ϕ transfers its quality to ω, and ω transfers neither quality nor quantity to ψ, but merely excites ψ – that is indicates the direction to be taken by the free psychical energy [of attention].

(*Origins*, p. 142)

Thus,

On this view, perceptual processes would *eo ipso* [from their very nature] involve consciousness, and would only produce further psychical effects *after* becoming conscious.

(ibid.)

It appears, thus, that it was Freud's interest in establishing that ω was moved by quality without any transfer of quantity which led him to place it between ϕ and ψ rather than to put ψ between ϕ and ω, since in the latter case he would have been forced either to transmit quantity from ϕ through ψ to ω or else he would have had to have quality pass from ϕ to ψ to ω and thus have quality in ψ. But in one instance Freud does have to provide for consciousness that reaches ω through ψ, this is in the awareness of pleasure and pain and word images from within, and as we shall see in the next section, this calls for another revision in the relationship between ϕ, ψ and ω. But in the *Project*, the issue of perceiving states of internal origin appears to pose no insurmouutable problem:

Besides the series of sensory qualities, it [*perception*] exhibits another series very different from that – the series of sensations of *pleasure* and *unpleasure*. . . . the hypothesis would follow that when the level in ψ rises the cathexis in ω increases, and when, on the other hand, that level falls, the cathexis diminishes. Pleasure and unpleasure would be the sensations in ω of its own cathexis, of its own level. . . . In this manner, the quantitative processes in ψ too would reach consciousness, once more as qualities.

(S.E., p. 312)

We have already noted in Chapter 1 that Freud would have saved himself and everyone else a great deal of confusion if he had from the beginning separated the quantitative concepts of drive, energy and effort from the qualitative concepts of unpleasure and pleasure. After all, we are able to perceive the difference between hunger and sleepiness, between sexiness and thirst, between fear, hate, love and attraction, not only between pleasure and unpleasure (anxiety). Here, he acknowledges the problem but does not really provide a mechanism for its solution. Nor is such a solution achieved in subsequent theorizing: for instance, combining the scheme in the *Project* with that of the later letter, Freud wrote in *The Interpretation of Dreams*:

Excitatory material flows into the Cs. [*consciousness*] sense-organ from two directions: from the Pcpt. [*perceptual*] system, whose excitation, determined by qualities, is probably submitted to a fresh revision [*through the mechanism of attention*] before it becomes a conscious sensation, and from the interior of the apparatus [*the brain's ψ system*] itself, *whose quantitative processes are felt qualitatively in the pleasure-unpleasure series* [*emphasis ours*] when, subject to certain modifications [*the mechanism of satisfaction by way of reality testing*], they make their way to consciousness.

(*The Interpretation of Dreams*, S.E., vol. 5, pp. 615–16)

ATTENTION – A PREPERCEPTUAL HIERARCHY OF FEEDBACK MECHANISMS

By contrast to the failure to provide a clear qualitative (i.e. patterned) mechanism for the pleasure-unpleasure type of feelings, an outstanding contribution to cognitive theory appears in the *Project* as a detailed statement of the wealth of feedback mechanisms involving the 'central sense organs' which constitute the process of attention. When perceptions occur, the act of perceiving leads to a discharge which results in a stimulus which in turn affects the act of perceiving. The *Project* states:

In the case of every external perception a qualitative excitation occurs in ω [p. 309], which in the first instance, however, has no significance for ψ. It must be added that the ω excitation leads to ω discharge, and information of this, as of every discharge [p. 318], reaches ψ. *The information of the discharge from ω is thus the indication of quality or of reality for ψ.*

(S.E., p. 325)

Thus as a result of an 'indication of quality', stimuli are more vivid and therefore made available to processing.

Let us suppose that to begin with, the ego is not prepared in advance; a perceptual cathexis occurs and, after it, its indication of quality. The intimate facilitation between the two pieces of information will further increase the perceptual cathexis and now a cathexis of the perceptual neurones with attention will result. The next perception of the same object will (in accordance with the second law of association) lead to a fuller cathexis of the same perception and only this will be the perception that is serviceable psychically.

(S.E., p. 362)

Essentially, therefore, the *Project* contains a description of a feedback process originating in a discharge in ω to ψ which in turn leads to reinforcement of the cathexis in ω when the ψ stimulus feeds back, 'leads to a fuller cathexis', in ω. This feedback makes up what Freud calls the second biological rule:

... *the biological rule of attention* runs: *If an indication of reality appears, then the perceptual cathexis which is simultaneously present is to be hypercathected.*
This is the second biological rule. The first one was that *of primary defence.*

(S.E., p. 371)

The *Project* argues that attention 'is biologically justified'.

... I believe that it [*attention*] is biologically determined – that is, that it has been left over in the course of psychical evolution because any other behaviour by ψ has been excluded. ...

(S.E., p. 361)

The relationship between the variety of other ψ processes and attention is also detailed:

The outcome of *psychical attention* is the cathexis of the same neurones which are bearers of the perceptual cathexis. This state has a prototype in the *experience of satisfaction* [p. 318], which is so important for the whole course of development, and in its repetitions, states of *craving* which have developed into states of *wishing* and states of *expecting.*

(S.E., p. 361)

Further, the relationship to perception is made clear:

Attention thus consists in establishing the psychical state of expectation even for those perceptions which do not coincide [*even*] in part with wishful cathexes. For it has in fact become important for a cathexis to be sent to meet all perceptions, since those that are wished-for might be among them. *Attention* is biologically justified; it is only a question of guiding the ego as to *which* expectant cathexis it is to establish and this purpose is served by the indications of quality.

(S.E., p. 361)

Thus expectation is determined not only by the process of wishing but also by perceptions of reality:

As an outcome of biological experience, ψ attention is constantly directed to the indications of quality. These take place, therefore, on precathected neurones and with sufficiently great quantity. The information of quality, thus strengthened, strengthens the perceptual cathexes by its facilitation; and the ego has learnt to make its cathexes of attention follow the passage of this associative movement from the indication of quality to the perception. By this means it is led to cathect precisely the right perceptions or their environment. Indeed, if we assume that it is the same $Q\dot{\eta}$ from the ego which travels by the facilitation from the indication of quality to the perception, we have actually explained the cathexis of attention mechanically (automatically) [p. 360.] Thus attention leaves the indications of quality and turns to the now hypercathected perceptual neurones.

(S.E., p. 362)

The indication of reality directs a cathexis of attention to the percept. A more detailed statement would be that the percept leads to a discharge, which in turn results in a sensation (the indication of reality) which results in directing attention cathexis to the percept, reinforcing it.

The details of arrangement were made explicit in a diagram and letter of 6th December 1896 in which Freud describes three systems of transcription, unconscious, and preconscious, and conscious which later become two central 'sense organs' – separate but closely connected as steps in a hierachy which provides for the double feedback described above.

Pcpt.-s is the first registration of the perceptions; it is quite incapable of being conscious and is arranged according to associations of simultaneity.

Uc. (unconsciousness) is a second registration, or transcription, arranged according to other associations – perhaps according to causal relations. *Uc.* traces may correspond to conceptual memories; they too are inaccessible to consciousness.

Pc. (preconsciousness) is the third transcription, attached to verbal images and corresponding to the official ego. The cathexes proceeding from this *Pc.* become conscious in accordance with certain rules. This secondary 'thought-consciousness' is subsequent in time and is probably connected with the hallucinatory activation of verbal images; so that the neurones of consciousness would once again be perceptual neurones and in themselves devoid of memory. [Figure 4.]

(*Origins*, pp. 174–5)

Fig. 4. 'Pcpt.' = perception; 'Pcpt.-s.' = perceptual signs; 'Uc.' = unconscious (signs); 'Pc.' = preconscious (signs); 'Consc.' = consciousness. These abbreviations are the precursors of the familiar 'Ucs.', etc., which were first used in the letter to Fliess of 31 May 1897 (No. 64) and were introduced into Freud's published writings in Section B of the seventh chapter of *The Interpretation of Dreams* (1900).

These proposals certainly have a modern ring. Let us look in on a more recent account of the problem:

We must turn now . . . to more general conceptions of pattern recognition. . . . It is appropriate to begin with the work of Oliver Selfridge . . . Selfridge (1955, 1956) was one of the first workers in the computer field to recognize the complexity of the problem. . . . In 1959, he proposed a more systematic model for pattern recognition, called 'Pandemonium' . . . [which is represented in Figure 5]. In a Pandemonium, each possible pattern is represented by a demon (the 'cognitive demons,' in the upper row [Pcpt?] of Figure [5]). Being egotistic, such a demon incessantly looks for evidence

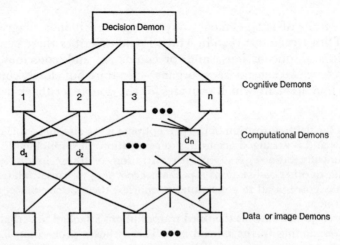

Fig. 5. Parallel processing in Selfridge's (1959) 'Pandemonium' programme.

(suitable results offered by inferior 'computational demons') that he is being depicted in the 'image', or input [Uc?]. To the extent that he finds such evidence, he shouts loudly, and the loudest shout in his Pandemonium is taken by the 'decision demon' as identifying the stimulus [Pc?]. The computational demons perform operations of varying complexity on the input, all simultaneously. . . .

The Pandemonium conception has been applied to several real problems in automatic pattern recognition, including the translation of hand-sent Morse code and the identification of hand-printed letters (see Selfridge and Neisser, 1960, for a summary of this work). In the case of hand-printed letters (Doyle, 1960), a system with about 30 rather complex feature-analyzers was simulated on a general-purpose computer. In operation, it was first presented with several hundred letters as examples from which to 'learn'. During this phase, each input was accompanied by its correct identification. In the test phase, unfamiliar letters . . . were presented and identified with close to 90 per cent accuracy.

(Neisser, 1967, pp. 74–6)

In the *Project*, indications of reality (match between Pcpt and Uc) direct a cathexis of attention to the percept; in Pandemonium a 'demon' looks for evidence that he is being depicted – the decision demon identifying the stimulus results from a match between various partial – i.e. computational – demons (feature analysers). These are all 'attentional' mechanisms which are critical to any comparative cognitive theories of perception. Neisser states the case as follows:

None of the theories considered . . . can do justice to human or even mech-anical pattern recognition, unless they are supplemented by some notion of 'attention'. There must be a way to concentrate the processes of analysis on a selected portion of the field. This implies that there are also 'preattentive processess': wholistic operations which form the units to which attention may then be directed, and which can directly control simple motor behavior. The act of attention itself is better thought of as 'constructive' than as 'analytic'.

(Neisser, 1967, pp. 74–86)

And then in the treatment of the mechanism of attention under the heading 'Focal Attention' we come upon the following passage:

The term 'focal attention' is taken from Schachtel, a psychoanalyst who has tried to account for the growing child's increasing interest in and under-standing of the real world without giving up the traditional analytic concern with affects and drives. A chief tool for this cognitive development is focal attention, '. . . man's capacity to center his attention on an object fully, so that he can perceive or understand it from many sides, as clearly as possible' (1959, p. 251). Of course, selective attention was not discovered by Schachtel; psychologists have discussed it for a century. Solley and Murphy (1960, Ch. 9) provide a historical review of the subject. Like most writers, they regard all attention as the manifestation of a single process, and as an allocation of 'energy'. However, the metaphor of energy has never been very enlightening where cognition is concerned. If even mechanical recognizers will need some such capacity to deal with complex problems, we had better abandon the energetic model and treat attention as an aspect of information-process-ing. (It is worth mentioning that, so far as I know, no existing computer program has this capacity. This is one reason why, except in highly specific applications, pattern recognition by machine is still greatly inferior to its human counterpart.)

It seems to me, therefore, that attention is not a mysterious concentration

95

of psychic energy; it is simply an allotment of analyzing mechanisms to a limited region of the field. To pay attention to a figure is to make certain analyses of, or certain constructions in, the corresponding part of the icon (representation).

(Neisser, 1967, pp. 88–9)

If Neisser had been acquainted with the *Project*, these statements about the 'metaphor of energy' would not have been necessary:

If I have on the one hand the ego and on the other hand perception – that is, cathexes in ψ coming from ϕ (from the external world) – then I require a mechanism which causes the ego to follow the perceptions and to influence them. I find it [such a mechanism] in the fact, that, according to my pre-suppositions, a perception invariably excites ω and thus gives rise to in-dications of quality. To put it more accurately, it excites consciousness (consciousness of quality) in ω, and the discharge of the ω excitation will, [like] every discharge, furnish information to ψ, which is in fact the in-dication of quality. I therefore put forward the suggestion that it is these indications of quality which *interest* ψ in the perception [cf. p. 335].
This would seem to be the mechanism of psychical attention.

(S.E., p. 360)

Thus a double feedback process is described in the *Project* – so important is it that Freud explicitly replies to the notion that one feedback ought to suffice. He first raises and answers the objection for external perception:

It may now be objected that a mechanism like this with the help of the indications of quality is redundant. The ego might have learnt biologically itself to cathect the perceptual region in states of expectation, instead of only being induced to make this cathexis by the indications of quality. There are, however, two things to be said here in justification of the mechanism of attention. (1) The region of the indications of discharge from ω is obviously a smaller one, comprises fewer neurones, than that of the perceptions – that is, of the whole pallium of ψ which is connected with the sense organs [p. 315]; so that the ego saves an extraordinarily large expenditure by keeping the indications of discharge cathected instead of the perceptions. And (2) the indications of discharge or indications of quality are first and foremost also indications of reality, which should precisely serve the purpose of distinguishing real perceptual cathexes from wishful cathexes. Thus we cannot evade the mechanism of attention. But it consists, in every case, of the ego *cathecting* those *neurones*, in which a cathexis has already appeared.

(S.E., p. 371)

The issue as to whether the entire input (perceptual region) is to be

96

attended is again a current one. Let us once more see how Neisser handles it in a contemporary text on cognitive processes:

Since the processes of focal attention cannot operate on the whole visual field simultaneously, they can come into play only after the preliminary operations have already segregated the figural units involved. These preliminary operations are of great interest in their own right. They correspond in part to what Gestalt psychologists called 'autochthonous forces', and they produce what Hebb called 'primitive unity'. I will call them the *preattentive processes* to emphasize that they produce the objects which later mechanisms are to flesh out and interpret.

The requirements of this task mean that the preattentive processes must be genuinely 'global' and 'wholistic'. Each figure or object must be separated from the others in its entirety, as a potential framework for the subsequent and more detailed analyses of attention. However, processes can be 'global' without being mysterious, or even very subtle. Very simple operations can separate units, provided they have continuous contours or empty spaces between them. Computer programs which follow lines or detect gaps, for example, are as easily written as those which fill holes and wipe out local irregularities. (Those who prefer analog to digital models, for physiological reasons, may note that similar forms of organization can be achieved by chemical and electrical field processes. These were the models preferred by the Gestalt psychologists; e.g., Köhler, 1924.)

For the most part, I will treat the preattentive processes as if they were a single level of operations, themselves parallel, serving to form the objects of focal attention. But this is an oversimplification; even these early processes can apparently have hierarchical depth. On request, you can focus your attention onto a single letter of the page (for example, the *q* which occurred earlier in this sentence). Having found it, you can note whether it is well formed, or how it differs from such letters as *p* and *b*. The preattentive processes keep the *q* a separate and integral unit while you do so. This is an acquired skill, very difficult for young children and illiterates. They must get along with much more crude objects of attention, such as the entire block of print on the page, or the whole word in which the *q* is embedded. Thus it would be a mistake to assume that the preattentive mechanisms of figural unity are all innate, although some of them must be.

. . . Attentive acts are [thus] carried out in the context of the more global properties already established at the preattentive level. In this way – and I think only in this way – can we understand the phenomena stressed by the Gestalt psychologists. In terms of information processing, the whole is *prior* to its parts.

(Neisser, 1967, pp. 89–91)

COMPARING AND JUDGING

We are now in a position to discuss the mechanism of judging. This process, which we previewed in Chapter 2, involves dividing a percept into a constant portion, a 'thing' or a 'subject', and a variable portion, a 'predicate', 'attribute', or 'activity', and it is the *variable portion which can be 'understood'* because by a process of comparison it is found to coincide with 'bodily experiences, sensations, and motor images of one's own' (S.E., p. 333). Freud makes the point several times in various parts of the *Project* and because of its central importance we shall quote them all:

The perceptual complex, if it is compared with other perceptual complexes, can be dissected into a component portion, neurone *a*, which on the whole remains the same, and a second component portion, neurone *b*, which for the most part varies. Language will later apply the term *judgement* to this dissection and *will discover the resemblance which in fact exists between the nucleus of the ego and the constant perceptual component [on the one hand] and between the changing cathexes in the pallium [pp. 315 and 323] and the inconstant component* [on the other] [*emphasis ours*]; it [language] will call neurone *a* the *thing* and neurone *b* its activity or attribute – in short, its *predicate* [cf. pp. 331–2, 366 and 383].

(S.E., p. 328)

Compare this with Neisser's statement of the same issue:

Following the preattentive mechanisms comes the second level of pattern analysis, which operates on the 'objects' segregated by the first. Here it is determined that an object is 'round and nubbly in texture', or a triangle, or a long-lost friend. These operations necessarily come after the preattentive ones and depend on them.

(Neisser, 1967, pp. 89–90)

What is called preattentive, attentive and cognitive (judgemental) are different in the different treatments of the issue, but the mechanisms proposed are remarkably similar. Freud, however, places more emphasis on 'memories of movements of one's own body' than most contemporary cognitive theorists, although Gibson (1966) has recently remarked on the importance of this aspect of perception and *Gestalt* oriented theories such as those of Werner and Wapner (1952) have repeatedly returned to it. In the *Project*, the mechanism is portrayed explicitly:

Then the perceptual complexes proceeding from this fellow human-being will in part be new and non-comparable – his *features*, for instance, in the visual sphere; but other visual perceptions – e.g., those of the movements of his hands – will coincide in the subject with memories of quite similar visual impressions of his own, of his own body, [memories] which are associated with memories of movements experienced by himself. Other perceptions of the object too – if, for instance, he screams – will awaken the memory of his [the subject's] own screaming and at the same time of his own experiences of pain. Thus the complex of the fellow human-being falls apart into two components, of which one makes an impression by its constant structure and stays together as a *thing*, while the other can be *understood* by the activity of memory – that is, can be traced back to information from [the subject's] own body. This dissection of a perceptual complex is described as *cognizing* it; it involves a judgement and when this last aim has been attained it comes to an end.

(S.E., p. 331)

So judging is the process by which cognition is performed. And:

At the start of the function of judgement, when the perceptions, on account of their possible connection with the wished-for object, are arousing interest, and their complexes (as has already been shown [pp. 328 and 331–2]) are dissected into an unassimilable component (the thing) and one known to the ego from its own experience (attribute, activity) – [*this is*] what we call *understanding*. . . .

(S.E., p. 366)

So understanding is related to judging, with the difference that it is only the variable portion which is understood. And:

The ego arrived at this through a discovery in its organization – through the fact already mentioned [pp. 331 and 366] that perceptual cathexes coincide in part with information from one's own body. As a consequence, the perceptual complexes are divided into a constant, non-understood, part – the *thing* – and a changing, understandable, one – the attribute or movement of the thing. Since the thing-complex recurs linked with a number of attribute-complexes, and these recur linked with a number of thing-complexes, a possibility arises of working out the pathways of thought leading from these two kinds of complex to the wished-for state of the thing, [and of doing so] in a manner which is, as it were, valid generally and without regard to the perception which is the real one at the moment.

(S.E., pp. 383–4)

Here again, the analysis presented in the *Project* resonates with current interest. The usage of terms may differ somewhat, but the issues are the same. Thus Neisser presents the case as follows:

. . . The concept of figural synthesis may help to clarify the phenomenon often called 'physiognomic' perception (Werner, 1948, p. 69; Koffka, 1935, p. 359). Everyone has perceived such traits as suppressed anger in a face, gaiety in a movement, or peaceful harmony in a picture. Often these perceptions seem

99

very direct. We do not first notice the tightness of the jaw and then infer the anger; more often it is the other way around. Such reactions are not so rare that cognitive psychology can afford to ignore them. According to many developmental psychologists, they are the rule rather than the exception in children. There is no doubt that they can become excruciatingly powerful in particular psychoses, and under the influence of certain drugs. Under some conditions every visible object may take on a menacing or a horrifying or a lewd appearance; it may also happen that everything seems beautiful and graceful beyond all description. Such emotion-flooded experiences can be thought of as the result of particular kinds of construction.

(Neisser, 1967, pp. 95-7)

With respect to cognitive terminology, we must recall that Freud is responsible for the term 'agnosia', a deficit in cognitive (gnostic) processes due to brain pathology, and its current universal usage in clinical neurology. Agnosia is defined as an inability to identify objects and there have been decades of neuropsychological experiments devoted to analysing its genesis. These have recently been reviewed by one of us in a paper entitled 'The Amnestic Syndromes' (Pribram, 1969), as demonstrating a distinction between context free 'sign' constructions by way of the attributes of 'things' and context sensitive 'symbolic' constructions leading to symbols or tokens of things (see also Pribram, 1971). But a full discussion of the process of symbolization as it is presented in the *Project* would get us ahead of our story, and is taken up in Chapter 4.

REALITY TESTING

We must first dispose of the issues of reality testing and the ability of organisms to perform specific actions. Perhaps the most important discussion of feedback in the *Project* is the description of reality testing – a part of the process of satisfaction so necessary, as we saw in the last chapter, to the development and maintenance of the structure of the ego. Recall that:

The total event [*e.g. as produced by the intervention of a caretaking person*] then constitutes an *experience of satisfaction*. . . . For three things occur in the ψ system: (1) a lasting discharge is effected and so the urgency which had produced unpleasure in ω is brought to an end; (2) a cathexis of one (or several) of the neurones which correspond to the perception of an object occurs in the pallium; and (3) at other points of the pallium information arrives of the discharge of the released reflex movement which follows upon the specific action. A facilitation is then formed between these cathexes and the nuclear neurones.

(S.E., p. 318)

More detail is presented in neurological terms:

... the wishful cathexis relates to neurone a + neurone b, and the perceptual cathexis to neurone $a + c$ ... the activity of the ego follows the connections of this neurone c and, by means of a current of $Q\dot{\eta}$ along these connections, causes new cathexes to emerge until access is found to the missing neurone b.

(S.E., pp. 327–8)

The aim is to go back to the missing neurone b and to release the sensation of identity – that is, the moment at which only neurone b is cathected, at which the travelling cathexis debouches into neurone b [cf. pp. 332 and 378].

(S.E., p. 329)

This is the identity which was established when the first successful gratification took place. And this aim to achieve identity is the model of the seventh chapter of *The Interpretation of Dreams*, too, where it is extended from primary to identities established by secondary processes:

The primary process endeavours to bring about a discharge of excitation in order that, with the help of the amount of excitation thus accumulated, it may establish a 'perceptual identity' [with the experience of satisfaction . . .]. The secondary process, however, has abandoned this intention and taken on another in its place – the establishment of a *'thought* identity' [with that experience].

(*The Interpretation of Dreams*, S.E., vol. 5, p. 602)

It seems clear that the model of *The Interpretation of Dreams* is in fact a comparison-through-feedback model, just as is the model of the *Project*.

It is important to realize that the process of comparison between a percept and the memory of a gratifying object represents one type of *judging activity*. It was actually in connection with such comparison that Freud first described judging (see S.E., vol. 1, pp. 330–31).

Even in the *Project*, Freud wished to make clear that, for the most part, judgement is not a 'primary function', a discharge mechanism, because there has to be some cathexis of the unfamiliar, the 'thing' or 'subject':

Judgement, as will be seen, is not a primary function, but presupposes the cathexis from the ego of the disparate [non-comparable] portions [of the perception]. In the first instance it has no practical purpose. . . .

(S.E., p. 332)

101

However, judging is initially a primary *process*, a process in which associative mechanisms predominate.

> In this [in primary judging] it is a matter of pursuing an association which is due to partial coincidence [between the wishful and perceptual cathexes] – an association to which no modification is applied. And indeed, cases also occur in which the associative process of judging is carried out with a full [amount of] quantity.
>
> (S.E., p. 333)

Freud describes these latter instances as taking place during primitive 'imitation' and as the 'sympathetic value' of a perception, the first referring to copying a movement and the second to feeling unpleasure at perceiving it. He refers in a quotation we used earlier to these two kinds of judging as primary processes:

> In these two cases we must no doubt see the *primary process* in respect of judging, and we may assume that all secondary judging has come about through a mitigation of these purely associative processes.
>
> (S.E., pp. 333–4)

One must take care not to become confused. Though judging has primary and secondary process forms, even primitive judging requires some ego cathexis. Clearly, there is a continuum; the distinction between primary and secondary process is not absolute.

He carried the analysis even further than we have already quoted it and wrote:

> The process can be analysed further. If neurone *a* coincides [in the two cathexes] but neurone *c* is perceived instead of neurone *b*, then the activity of the ego follows the connections of this neurone *c* and, by means of a current of $Q\dot\eta$ along these connections, causes new cathexes to emerge until access is found to the missing neurone *b*. As a rule, the image of a movement [a motor image] arises which is interpolated between neurone *c* and neurone *b*; and, when this image is freshly activated through a movement carried out really, the perception of neurone *b*, and at the same time the identity that is being sought, are established. Let us suppose, for instance, that the mnemic image wished for [by a child] is the image of the mother's breast and a front view of its nipple, and that the first perception is a side view of the same object, without the nipple. In the child's memory there is an experience, made by chance in the course of sucking, that with a particular head-movement the front image turns into the side image. The side image which is now seen leads to the [image of the] head-movement; an experiment shows that its counterpart must be carried out, and the perception of the front view is achieved.

There is not much judgement about this as yet; but it is an example of the possibility of arriving, by a reproduction of cathexes, at an action which is already one of the accidental offshoots of the specific action.

(S.E., pp. 328–9)

These procedures of comparison with subsequent operations to achieve identity – which Freud assumes to take place between excitations derived from memory traces and those derived from sensory inputs, and between these and those derived from head movements – again have a surprisingly modern ring. Neisser states the matter thus for cognitive psychology:

As noted earlier, the versatility of pattern recognition resembles our equally impressive ability to transfer a once-learned movement to any limb of the body. . . . Perceiving a letter and writing one are synthetic activities of the same kind.

(Neisser, 1967, p. 97)

And Pribram parallels this exposition of the problem in neuropsychology:

The problem is this. Because of the way in which motor systems are organized only one step of an action can be performed at a time. Yet when you or I sit down to write, or type, or speak, or play the piano, we have stored in our brains a considerably detailed representation of how the entire action is to be achieved. The evidence for such a stored representation comes from 'slips of the tongue' in speaking or 'slips of the fingers' in musical performances, inversions in the order of words in a sentence or letters in a word, the flexibility in the arrangement of the order in which thoughts are expressed on different occasions and the like. The problem is thus not completely unfamiliar. The question is what type of transfer function is involved when one representation is transformed by virtue of neural operations into another. This problem has already been met in earlier chapters [on perception].

(Pribram, 1971, pp. 217–19)

In short, perceiving, reality testing, is a skill akin to and an important part of the development of intentional, willed, i.e. specific, actions taken by the organism on the basis of his memory-motive (wishful) and ego processes. Let us therefore pursue the organization of the processes that lead to action.

ACTION

Feedback, circular, reflex, processes abound in the nervous system and Freud was not unaware of this fact when he constructed his model. The metapsychological model, first described in the *Project*, is laced throughout with these loops. A distinction must here be made, however, between a reflex (re-flux and re-flection) and the neural reflex-arc model suggested by Sherrington (1947) to account for spinal reflexes. He invoked a stimulus-response sequence without feedback to account for the spinal reflex. Sherrington, however, failed to take into consideration a large group (1/3 by volume) of efferent (motor) fibres in the ventral root which terminate not in contractile muscle but in muscle spindle stretch receptors. Thus the reflex-arc concept has to be modified in favour of a feedback mechanism. The implications of this modification have been set forth in detail in two volumes, the first, *Plans and the Structure of Behavior*, by Miller, Galanter and Pribram (1960), where a Test-Operate-Test-Exit (TOTE) replacement for the reflex arc was initially presented (Ch. 4), and the second, *Languages of the Brain* (Pribram, 1971), where the ramifications of neuropsychological data and theory bearing on this change in principle have been pursued (Ch. 5; Part III).

Thus the distinction between reflex and reflex arc rests on the fact that the effects of an activity reflect *back* on the input that initiated the activity and thus modify it. Today the term 'feedback' is commonly used where the more general 'reflex' would have served in the eighteenth and nineteenth centuries. Feedback or servomechanisms as such were not, of course, recognized then; nor were the formal properties of control worked out. But in several aspects of Freud's *Project* these developments were anticipated in a relatively sophisticated fashion. One we have already met: the complex of structure which guides drive, drive restraint and drive discharge. In the *Project*, as we have seen, a positive feedback mechanism involves chemical substances secreted by key neurons which, in turn, stimulate the increase of other substances to which the nervous system is sensitive. This produces an accrual, a continual augmentation of excitation which must be inhibited if the human machine is not to explode. We have suggested that current neurophysiology would substitute a negative for the positive feedback loop but would not alter the conception of a hierarchy of control achieved by the development of a facilitatory memory-motive and an inhibitory delay system (the ego) which can store and then get rid of excitation in appropriately timed, graded, amounts.

In this chapter we have met a second major use of feedback in the detailing of the mechanism of attention in the process of reality testing. Yet a third use is with regard to motor phenomena. Motor phenomena play a vital role in the psychoanalytic model, as of course they must in any comprehensive theory of behaviour. For motor function, feedbacks occur when the behaviour of the organism initiates signals to the organism, as a result of which the behaviour can be modified if necessary. When the behaviour comprises movement, the motion results in a sensation which is used to check the accuracy of the motion. Freud wrote in the *Project*:

. . . every movement, through its subsidiary results, becomes the occasion for fresh sensory excitations (from the skin and muscles) which give rise to a *motor* [kinaesthetic] *image* in ψ.

(S.E., p. 318)

We note here that the motor image is composed of feedback signals, since it is the sensory excitation that results from discharge: 'Motor images are sensory' (p. 387) – a most succinct statement of feedback. The last paragraph of the *Project* concerns itself with motor *images*. Since these are sensory they do have quality and can arouse consciousness, sometimes even attracting great attention.

Their qualities, however, are not very striking, and probably not so multifarious as those of the external world; and they are not associated with word-presentations but on the contrary, they themselves serve in part the purposes of that association.

(S.E., p. 387)

This is, of course, a reference to the issue of speech, q.v. Chapter 4. The explanation of the nature of the quality of motor images is that they do not arise from highly organized sense organs.

Motor images are important because they become transformed in the production of action. A relatively formal definition and description of action appears near the end of the *Project*:

Action . . . we can only picture as the [*result of*] full cathexis of those motor images which have been brought into prominence during the thought process [p. 384 f.], in addition . . . to those which (if there was a state of expectation) formed part of the volitional component . . .

(S.E., p. 386)

Note the reference to the volitional, intentional, willed component of the action, noted in Chapter 1 and earlier in this chapter to be the secondary process equivalent of wish. That secondary, intentional processes are involved is made clear by the fact that the ψ system is not completely discharged – a point which is related to the need for secondary processes in ψ to maintain a constant store of energy. The distinction between the primary process of wishing and the secondary

105

process of intentional willing is even more fully described in later writings:

A new function was now allotted to motor discharge, which, under the dominance of the pleasure principle, had served as a means of unburdening the mental apparatus of accretions of stimuli, and which had carried out this task by sending innervations into the interior of the body (leading to expressive movements and the play of features and to manifestations of affect). Motor discharge was now employed in the appropriate alteration of reality; it was now converted into *action*.

> (*Formulations on the Two Principles of Mental Functioning*, 1911,
> S.E., vol. 12, p. 221)

Here we thus have succinctly described the distinction between motor discharge, a primary, and action, a secondary process. This distinction has been validated by a considerable number of neurophysiological and neurobehavioural experiments as has been detailed elsewhere by Pribram (1971, Chs. 13, 14). Essentially, primary process motor discharge involves coordinated muscle contractions, movements which are undisturbed by resections of the precentral motor cortex of the brain. Such resections do, however, impair specific, secondary processes, actions, by virtue of the fact that 'images' of the forces involved in such actions are disrupted:

In summary, the neural control of behavior is achieved largely through an effect on receptor functions. At the reflex level, receptor sensitivity to the imposition of load initiates and guides an adaptive counter-process in the servomechanism. The sum of such adaptations constitutes the background tonic steady state against which new adjustments occur. Large-scale adjustments such as changes in posture are controlled by the basal ganglia-anterior cerebellar (extrapyramidal) system of the brain, while more discrete movements such as typing or playing the piano are regulated by a fast-time extrapolatory computation carried on by the neocerebellar system. The precise mechanism of these central controls has yet to be worked out, but we know enough to ascertain that patterning of the peripheral servomechanisms is involved, and that this patterning is achieved by changing the mechanism's bias. Finally, the conception of the functions of the cerebral motor cortex of the precentral gyrus has radically changed. This part of the brain cortex has been shown to be the sensory cortex for action. A momentary Image-of-Achievement is constructed and continuously updated through a neural . . . process much as is the perceptual Image. The Image-of-Achievement is, however, composed of learned anticipations of the force and changes in force required to perform a task. These fields of force exerted on muscle receptors become the parameters of the servomechanism and are directly (via the thalamus) and indirectly (via the basal ganglia and cerebellum) relayed to the motor cortex, where they are correlated with a fast-time cerebellar computation to predict the outcomes of the next steps of the action. When the course of action becomes reasonably predictable from the trends of prior successful predictions, a terminal Image-of-Achievement can be constituted to serve as a guide for the final phases of the activity.

(Pribram, 1971, pp. 249–50)

Compare this account with the one provided in the *Project*:

During the action, therefore, a fresh comparison must be made between the information which arrives of movements and the precathected [movements] [*motor images*], and there must be an excitation of correcting innervations till identity is achieved. The same thing is repeated here which occurred on the perceptual side, though with less multiplicity, more rapidity and continuous *full* discharge, which was absent in the other instance [in that of perceptions]. The analogy, however, between practical thought and expedient action is noteworthy. We can see from it that motor images are *sensory*.

(S.E., p. 387)

There is much richer detail and more complete understanding today, especially of the variables that produce a 'motor image', but the problems that must be faced are discernible in the *Project*.

Critical to the whole conception of specific actions, however, is another rather different set of issues, those concerning implicit actions in the form of thought and explicit acts demanding a minimal expenditure of energy – the actions involved in speech. These specific actions involve even more circuitous neural constructions and form the topics of the next chapter.

[4]

THE THEORY OF
THOUGHT

THINKING – A SECONDARY PROCESS

The model delineated in the *Project* achieves nuances beyond those
presented thus far. To appreciate them, Freud's contribution to the
psychology of the thinking process must now be discussed in detail.
It is of considerable theoretical interest that at this point, though the
neurological mechanisms spelled out thus far are utilized, the burden
of analysis comes more and more to rest on the cognitive process *per se*.
We are now leaving the wetware of the brain to analyse the type of
programmes processed and the use to which they may be put. With
few exceptions, such as the work of Bartlett (1958) who considers, as
does Freud, thinking in terms of the development of a skilled performance, contemporary cognitive theory of thinking is in its infancy and
revolves almost completely around computer simulations of logical
problem solving processes. Reitman (1965) has reviewed these thoroughly and they have little relation to the proposals presented in the
Project which concern human thinking, much of which appears to be
non-logical, i.e. its constraints differ from those usually operating in the
solution of problems in logic where computers are especially effective.

Thought, as described in the *Project*, is a secondary process function
and therefore distinguished from the primary process 'succession of
associations':

The struggle between the established facilitations and the changing cathexes
is characteristic of the secondary process of reproductive thought, in contrast
to the primary sequence of association.

(S.E., p. 329)

And again:

The example of judgement gives us for the first time a hint of the difference in their quantitative characteristic which is to be discovered between thought and the primary process.

(S.E., p. 334)

Judgement, the basis for one of the varieties of thought, can, as we have seen, also occur as a secondary process:

Thus judging is a ψ process which is only made possible by inhibition by the ego. . . .

(S.E., p. 328)

The major metapsychological hypotheses about thinking are already present in the *Project*. Thought is experimental action:

. . . *judging* . . . is evoked by the dissimilarity between the *wishful cathexis* of a memory and a perceptual cathexis that is similar to it. It can be inferred from this that coincidence between the two cathexes becomes a biological signal for ending the act of thought and for allowing discharge to begin. Their non-coincidence gives the impetus for the activity of thought, which is terminated once more with their coincidence.

(S.E., p. 328)

It is carried out with small quantities of energy:

It is probable that in the process of thought the displacement-quantities too are not large.

(S.E., p. 368)

The reasons that the quantities have to be small are the same as those given in *The Interpretation of Dreams*. In the *Project* Freud states:

In the first place, the expenditure of large $Q\dot\eta$ is a loss for the ego which has to be restricted as far as possible; for the $Q\dot\eta$ is ear-marked for the exacting specific action [pp. 297 and 323]. In the second place, a large $Q\dot\eta$ would pass along several associative pathways simultaneously and leave no time for thought-cathexis and would also cause a large expenditure.

(S.E., p. 368)

This conservation of quantity has its own important consequences:

But it is also clear that at the same time enough $Q\dot\eta$ is economized by [*the inhibition imposed by lateral cathexes*] to make the reproduction profitable as a whole. Otherwise, *all* the $Q\dot\eta$, which is finally needed for discharge, would be given off at the points of motor outlet during the course of its passage.

(S.E., p. 334)

About this profitable reproduction, the *Project* states:

. . . an opportunity arises for shortening the practical thought-process itself. For if it has turned out that the pathway from perception to identity with the wishful cathexis leads by way of a motor image M, then it is biologically ensured that after identity has been achieved this M will be fully innervated. Owing to the simultaneity of the perception and this M, an intense facilitation develops between the two of them, and an immediately subsequent perceptual image will arouse the M without any further passage of association. . . . What was originally a laboriously established thought-connection afterwards becomes, owing to simultaneous full cathexis, a powerful facilitation. The only question about it is whether it is always effected along the pathway that was first discovered or whether a more direct connection may be followed. The latter seems more likely and more expedient, since it spares the necessity for fixing pathways of thought which should, indeed, remain free for other connections of the most various kinds. If the [original] pathway of thought is not followed again, no facilitation of it is to be expected either, and the outcome will be better fixed by a more direct connection. It remains an open question, incidentally, whence the new pathway would originate. If the two cathexes, the perception and M, had a common association with a third one, the problem would be simplified.

(S.E., pp. 384-5)

In short, thinking is considered a secondary process which recapitulates earlier facilitations but with smaller quantities. The mechanism by which this comes about is detailed in full:

It is justifiable to suppose that during *thought* a slight current of motor innervation passes from ψ – only, of course, if during the process a motor or key neurone [p. 320] has been innervated. Nevertheless, it would be wrong to take this discharge for the process of thought itself, of which it is only an unintended subsidiary effect. The *process of thought* consists in the cathexis of ψ neurones, accompanied by a change, brought about by side-cathexis from the ego, in what is imposed by the facilitations. It is intelligible from the mechanical point of view that here only a part of the $Q\dot{\eta}$ is able to follow the facilitations and that the magnitude of this part is constantly regulated by the cathexes. But it is also clear that at the same time enough $Q\dot{\eta}$ is economized by this to make the reproduction profitable as a whole. Otherwise, *all* the $Q\dot{\eta}$, which is finally needed for discharge, would be given off at the points of motor outlet during the course of its passage. *Thus the secondary process is a repetition of the original ψ passage* [of quantity], *at a lower level, with smaller quantities.*

'With $Q\dot{\eta}$s even smaller', it will be objected, 'than those that ordinarily pass through in ψ neurones? How can it be arranged that such small $Q\dot{\eta}$s shall have open to them pathways which, after all, are only traversable by larger ones than ψ as a rule receives?' The only possible reply is that this must be a mechanical result of the side-cathexes. We must conclude that matters stand in such a way that when there is a side-cathexis small $Q\dot{\eta}$s flow through facilitations which would ordinarily be traversed only by large ones. The side-cathexis as it were *binds* a quota of the $Q\dot{\eta}$ flowing through the neurone.

There is a further condition that thought must satisfy. It must make no essential change in the facilitations created by the primary process; otherwise, indeed, it would falsify the traces of reality. Of this condition it is enough to remark that facilitation is probably the result of a single [passage of a] major quantity and that cathexis, though very powerful at the moment, nevertheless does not leave any comparable lasting effect behind it. The small Qs that pass during thought cannot in general prevail against the facilitations.

There is no doubt, however, that the process of thought does leave lasting traces behind it, since a second thinking, a rethinking, calls for so much less expenditure [of energy] than a first. In order that reality shall not be falsified, therefore, special traces are needed, signs of the processes of thought, constituting a thought-memory which it is not yet possible to shape. We shall hear later by what means the traces of thought-processes are distinguished from those of reality.

(S.E., pp. 334-5)

Note here the emphasis on ever smaller quantities involved in the thought process. In contemporary terms we would argue that thinking becomes progressively more an information processing rather than an error processing mechanism. But, as we shall presently see, error processing (primary processing) attributes of thinking are not abandoned completely. There are proposed mechanisms that deal with the corrective functions of thought.

TYPES OF THINKING

Thus, thinking is not conceived in the *Project* as a simple secondary process that displays a unitary organization. Freud defined and related to one another a number of kinds of thinking, in an analysis which, like so many other topics we have already touched upon, is carried out in the *Project* more comprehensively and subtly than in any of his subsequent writings.

The discussion is not simple to follow; at first a multiple and often seemingly contradictory terminology plagues the reader. Freud variously discusses practical, reproductive, recollecting, reflecting, ordinary, judging, observing, cognitive, theoretical and critical thinking. The difficulties, though never completely dispelled, are resolved to a considerable degree if one holds the hypothesis that Freud makes two major distinctions in his discourse. The first of these relates to the fact that some thinking is principally devoted to the exploration of an externally derived percept, while other thinking is principally devoted to the reproduction of past memories. To ease the terminological difficulty we will use Freud's terms observant and reproductive thought to explicate this distinction. Observant thinking is also called judgemental by Freud; reproductive thought is often coupled to reflection by him. The second distinction is founded on the idea that some thinking is guided by a wishful aim, while other thinking is not. We will use Freud's terms practical and critical thinking to pursue this distinction. The types of thinking based on these two distinctions become arranged in a variety of combinations. As we shall see, for instance, theoretical thinking involves an observant process applied to a train of reproductive thought, and so on. The complex combinations can be a source of confusion unless the original distinctions are kept clearly in mind and the possibility for combination is realized.

Either observant or reproductive thought can be involved in reality testing. Observant thought occurs when the wish is held constant and the perceptual cathexis is explored for possible coincidences:

. . . there is a wishful cathexis and a perception emerges which does not coincide in any way with the wished-for mnemic image (mnem.+). Thereupon there arises an interest for *cognizing* this perceptual image, so that it may perhaps after all be possible to find a pathway from it to mnem.+. . . . If the perceptual image is not absolutely new, it will now *recall* and *revive* a mnemic perceptual image with which it coincides at least partly.

(S.E., p. 330)

As to the necessity for investigating every path:

Now it is clearly the intention of *observing thought* to become acquainted to the furthest possible extent with the pathways leading from the perception; in this manner, indeed, knowledge of the perceptual object is to be made exhaustive.

(S.E., p. 364)

Most often opposed to observant thinking is reproductive thought. Here, the percept is not explored; rather the memory-images associated with the wish are surveyed:

. . . *reproductive* thought seeks it [*an identity with a perceptual image*] with a psychical cathexis of one's own (an experience of one's own.)

(S.E., p. 332)

Reproductive thinking is a term commonly employed and there are passages which seem to indicate that it is a synonym for practical thinking (which see below):

Thus reproductive thought has a practical aim and a biologically established end – namely to lead a $Q\dot{\eta}$, which is travelling from the superfluous [unwanted] perception, back to the cathexis of the missing neurone.

(S.E., p. 330)

But there is other evidence that the two are not equated. To begin with, Freud describes 'an aimless activity of memory' (S.E., p. 331) which is also characterized as 'reproductive consideration' (S.E., p. 332), and since practical thinking has been defined as directed by an aim, an aimless form of thinking cannot be practical thinking. More explicitly, however, Freud wrote:

Alongside of *cognitive [critical]* and practical thought, we must distinguish a reproductive, *remembering* thought, which in part enters into practical thought, but does not exhaust it.

(S.E., p. 379)

And soon thereafter:

This *remembering* is a precondition of all testing by critical thought. . . .

(S.E., p. 379)

About this we shall hear more. It is clear that reproduction may be a part of practical thought, of critical thought, or an aimless activity of recollection not clearly in the service either of a wishful cathexis or of a perception.

This last kind of reproductive thought is defined not only in the passages describing an 'aimless activity of memory' or 'reproductive reflection' but also in these:

The process [*of reproductive thinking which has a practical purpose*] can, however, make itself independent of this latter aim and strive only for identity. If so, we have before us a pure act of thought, though this can in any case be put to practical use later.

(S.E., p. 330)

And:

. . . the whole thought-process is able to make itself independent of the expectational process and of reality and is able to advance in a quite un-altered manner [*until*] identity [*is produced*]. Thus it starts from a mere *idea*, and, even after it is completed, does not lead to action; but it has produced a piece of *practical knowledge*, which can be used for a subsequent real occurrence.

(S.E., p. 378)

The *Project* also refers to the same kind of thinking as 'pure ψ activity, of reproductive remembering . . .' (S.E., p. 319).

This kind of thinking which reaches a piece of practical knowledge in advance of needing it is described as having two major advantages:

It is an obvious advantage if the arranging of thought, which takes place in practical thought, need not wait to occur till the state of expectation [*is set*] but can have occurred already [p. 378]: because (1) this will save time for the specific action to take shape [p. 378], (2) the state of expectation is far from being particularly favourable for the passage of thought. The value of promptitude in the short interval between perception and action is shown when we consider that perceptions change rapidly. If the thought-process lasts too long, its product will have become useless in the meantime. For that reason we '*think ahead*'.

(S.E., p. 383)

The difference between observant and reproductive thinking is essentially discussed as thinking concerned with a percept in contradistinction to thinking concerned with memory traces. There is, however, another major dimension on which the two types of thinking are differentiated. Contrary to what one might expect on superficial reading, in reproductive thinking the associations which are reproduced are those of experiences the organism encountered in interaction with the outside world. In observant thinking the associations which are reproduced – at least in the genesis of observant thinking – are experiences of the subject's own body. It is not too easy to pick this point up in the *Project*, partly because the external experiences and the body experiences are both translated 'experience' in English, whereas the German in the first case is '*Erlebnis*' and in the second case '*Erfahrung*'. An external experience is also called a 'psychic' experience in contradistinction to a 'body' or somatic experience. Freud wrote:

Cognitive or *judging* [*critical*] thought seeks an identity with a bodily cathexis, *reproductive* thought seeks it with a psychical cathexis of one's own. . . .

(S.E., p. 332)

And:

As regards judging, there is further to be remarked that its basis is obviously the presence of bodily experiences, sensations and motor images of one's own.

(S.E., p. 333)

And again:

Thus judging, which is later a means for the *cognition* of an object that may possibly be of practical importance, is originally an associative process between cathexes coming from outside and arising from one's own body – an *identification of information or cathexes from φ and from within*.

(S.E., p. 334)

This issue is of crucial importance for two principal reasons: first, it means that normal perception is essentially observant, and second, it is an integral part of Freud's hypothesis that observation is first learned on other human beings, a fact of enormous importance in the development of 'object' relationships.

As to the first point, it will be recalled that in the passages already quoted about observant thought, it is coming to know an object, to perceive, which stands in the foreground. Even more explicitly Freud wrote:

The perception may correspond to an object-nucleus + a motor image. While one is perceiving the perception, one copies the movement oneself – that is, one innervates so strongly the motor image of one's own which is aroused towards coinciding [with the perception], that the movement is carried out. Hence one can speak of a perception having an *imitation-value*. Or the perception may arouse the mnemic image of a sensation of pain of one's own, so that one feels the corresponding unpleasure and repeats the appropriate defensive movement. Here we have the *sympathy-value* of a perception.

(S.E., p. 333)

And then again:

In virtue of the trend towards *imitation*, which emerges during judging. . . .

(S.E., p. 367)

The argument that the first observations are those of other human beings follows from the fact that a percept – for early observations at any rate – can be meaningful only if it corresponds to some body experience of one's own, and this is called 'understanding' something:

. . . its basis is obviously the presence of bodily experiences, sensations and motor images of one's own. So long as these are absent, the variable portion [p. 328] of the perceptual complex remains ununderstood – that is, it can be reproduced but does not point a direction for further paths of thought.

(S.E., p. 333)

Since the first 'understandings' of this sort are based on one's own body experiences, the first perceptions which one will understand are those of similar bodily behaviours perceived in other human beings.

Freud adds, however, that the *interest* taken in other human beings – which is not the same as the capacity to understand a perception, though the quotation to follow does not separate these sharply enough – results from the fact that the first satisfying and the first hostile object is another human being:

Let us suppose that the object which furnishes the perception resembles the subject – a *fellow human-being*. If so, the theoretical interest [taken in it] is also explained by the fact that an object *like this* was simultaneously the [subject's] first satisfying object and further his first hostile object, as well as his sole helping power. For this reason it is in relation to a fellow human-being that a human-being learns to cognize.

(S.E., p. 331)

The second major distinction that underlies the many types of thinking discussed in the *Project* concerns the difference between practical or purposive and critical or theoretical thinking. '. . . practical thought lets itself be guided by the biological rule of defence' whereas in critical thought 'the rule is no longer observed' (S.E., p. 383).

There are obviously other kinds of thought-process which, instead of the disinterested aim of cognition, have another, practical, aim in view. The state of expectation, which was the starting-point of all thought [p. 361], is an example of this second kind of thought. Here a wishful cathexis is firmly retained, while alongside of it a second, perceptual, cathexis which emerges is followed with attention. But in this case the intention is not to discover in general where it will lead to, but to discover along what paths it will lead to the activation of the wishful cathexis which has meanwhile been firmly retained.

(S.E., p. 376)

We see then that practical thinking is guided from within, as it were, by the memory of satisfaction, but this is to repeat the formulation that it is guided by a wishful cathexis, while critical thinking is guided from outside, for it is led by the percept:

. . . it corresponds more or less to the state of an investigator who has made a perception and asks himself: what does this mean?

(S.E., p. 363)

Often Freud will speak of critical thought as cognitive, which term, in earlier passages of the *Project*, he had used more or less synonomously with judgemental or observational thinking. So, in these later passages, practical and cognitive become two terms commonly used to distinguish the two main kinds of thought:

With increasing memories fresh pathways of displacement are constantly appearing. For that reason it is found advantageous to follow the different perceptions completely in order among all the pathways to discover the most favourable; and this is the work of *cognitive* thought, which, to be sure, emerges as a preparation for practical [thought], though in fact it only developed out of the latter at a late stage. The results of this [work] are thereafter serviceable for more than one kind of wishful cathexis.

(S.E., p. 385)

And in his final statement dealing with the analysis of the type of thinking in the *Project*:

. . . [critical thought] is cognitive thought with a given object – namely, a series of thoughts.

(S.E., p. 386)

But what is a train of thought but reproductive reflection? In this way the distinctions which obtain originally become recombined as more complex ways of thinking are discussed. Yet, the initial distinctions are worth understanding completely. They again reflect Freud's propensity for stating the prospective and retrospective aspects of processes in his model separately: observant and practical thought are prospective in that they utilize the motive aspects of the wish to explore percepts and reality. By contrast, reproductive and critical thought are retrospective in that they analyse and modify the memory aspects of the memory-motive structure that comprises the wish.

ERRORS IN THINKING

An important area of investigation of thought processes is concerned with this modification of the memory-motive structure. In the *Project* this is detailed in a discussion of logical error. The organism is faced with the possibility that an error has occurred:

. . . when, in spite of all the rules having been observed, the process of expectation, followed by the specific action, leads to unpleasure instead of to satisfaction.

(S.E., p. 386)

There takes place then a particular kind of thought called:

Critical thought [*which*] seeks, without a practical aim, in a leisurely manner, and summoning up all the indications of quality, to repeat the whole passage of $Q\dot\eta$ in order to detect some *fault in thought* or some *psychological defect*.

(S.E., p. 386)

The *Project* defines 'critical thought' even more explicitly:

In thus following a backward direction, the process comes upon intermediate links which have hitherto been unconscious, which have left no indications of quality behind them but whose indications of quality appear subsequently.

(S.E., p. 379)

The distinction Freud makes between 'intellectual errors' and 'psychological defect' is that he regards all errors except logical errors

117

as due to psychological defects. These defects are grouped into those for critical thinking, for practical thinking and for thinking in general.

For critical thinking
1) Errors in making judgements:

For the thing-complex and movement-complex are never quite identical, and among their divergent components there may be some the neglect of which disturbs the outcome in reality. This defect in thought originates from the endeavour, which, indeed, we are copying here, to substitute a single neurone for the complex – which is necessitated precisely by the immense complexity.

(S.E., p. 384)

2) Errors due to failure in avoiding purposive aims:

The errors of cognitive [*critical*] thought are self-evident. They are partiality, where purposive cathexes have not been avoided, and incompleteness, where every pathway has not been followed.

(S.E., pp. 385–6)

For practical thinking
1) Errors may arise because the organism has not had enough experience – in the '*Erlebnis*' sense:

But no doubt an inexpedient pathway of thought may be entered upon and a wasteful movement emphasized, since with practical thought the choice is after all dependent only on reproducible experience.

With increasing memories fresh pathways of displacement are constantly appearing.

(S.E., p. 385)

2) Errors due to the fact that the expedient thought is too difficult in the face of old-established pattern:

An expenditure of this kind for overcoming good facilitations, in order to entice the Q along pathways which are worse facilitated but lie closer to the purposive cathexis, corresponds to difficulty in thinking.

(S.E., pp. 377–8)

For thinking in general
1) Errors due to ignorance:

. . . the perceptions of reality have not been completely perceived because they were not within range of the senses.

(S.E., p. 384)

2) Errors due to insufficient attention:

. . . the psychical precathexis may be defective (owing to the ego being deflected away from the perceptions) and inaccurate perceptions and incomplete passages of thought may result.

(S.E., p. 384)

3) Errors due to the generation of affect:

. . . the generation of affect inhibits the normal passage of thought, and in various ways. This happens, firstly, in that many paths of thought are forgotten which would ordinarily come into account – similarly, that is, to what occurs in dreams [p. 338]. . . . Secondly, [affect inhibits thought] in that without forgetting, pathways are followed which are ordinarily avoided: in particular, pathways leading to discharge, [such as] actions [performed] in the affect[ive state].

(S.E., p. 357)

And soon therefore:

Furthermore, the greater the quantity that is endeavouring to effect a passage, the harder for the ego is the activity of thought, which, as everything goes to show, consists in an experimental displacing of small $Q\dot{\eta}$s [p. 334 above and p. 367 ff. below]. 'Reflecting' is a time-consuming activity of the ego's, which cannot occur when there are strong $Q\dot{\eta}$s in the level of affect. That is why when there is affect there is over-hastiness, and a choice of pathways similar to the primary process.

(S.E., p. 358)

. . . but in what do *logical faults* consist? . . . in the non-observance of the *biological rules* for the passage of thought. These rules lay down where it is that the cathexis of attention is to be directed each time and when the thought-process is to come to a stop. They are protected by threats of unpleasure, they are derived from experience, and they can be transposed directly into the rules of logic – which will have to be proved in detail. Thus the intellectual unpleasure of contradiction, at which the passage of testing thought comes to a stop, is nothing other than the [unpleasure] accumulated for the protection of the biological rules, which is stirred up by an incorrect thought-process.

(S.E., p. 386)

And then Freud makes the extraordinary statement:

The existence of biological rules of this kind can in fact be proved from the feeling of unpleasure at logical faults.

(S.E., p. 386)

What is remarkable in this statement is that it applies the most basic laws according to which the psychic apparatus functions, the biological laws of attention and defence, to the highly complex process of logical thinking. Here one sees the extraordinary sweep and integration of the model.

The occasional departure from the biological rules by logical thinking is related to the important role played by preconscious thinking to which these rules are much less applicable. It is for these reasons that critical thought 'makes use to a large extent of indications of quality' (S.E., p. 379), for when thinking is conscious, the biological rules, especially that of attention, are much more likely to come into play. Thus the adaptive role of consciousness is underscored.

It will be recalled that:

In theoretical thought unpleasure plays no part, and it is therefore possible as well with tamed memories [*i.e. memories defended against by a well developed system of side-cathexes*].

(S.E., p. 386)

While this would seem to imply that tamed recollections release *no* unpleasure, the *Project* also contains the statement that:

In the course of this travelling it may happen that the $Q\dot{\eta}$ comes upon a memory which is connected with an experience of pain and thus gives occasion for a release of unpleasure. Since this is a sure sign that neurone *b* is not to be reached along that pathway, the current is at once diverted from the cathexis in question. Unpleasurable paths, however, retain their great value in directing the current of reproduction.

(S.E., pp. 329–30)

The integration of these two concepts of course lies in the 'signal' theory of anxiety:

Thus primary *thought-defence* arises, which, in practical thought, takes the release of unpleasure as a signal [p. 326] to leave a particular pathway – that is, to direct the cathexis of attention *elsewhere*.

(S.E., p. 382)

As already indicated:

. . . for with purposive thought it is a question of *some* pathway *or other* and, accordingly, those to which unpleasure attaches can be excluded; whereas with theoretical [thought] every pathway must be cognized.

(S.E., p. 383)

In *The Interpretation of Dreams*, Freud expressed the relevant proposition quite generally:

. . . thinking must aim at freeing itself more and more from exclusive regulation by the unpleasure principle and at restricting the development of affect in thought-activity to the minimum required for acting as a signal.

(S.E., vol. 5, p. 602)

But we cannot be sure that the generality of this statement means that Freud had decided it held for both cognitive and practical thinking, for the seventh chapter of *The Interpretation of Dreams* does not include the detailed and careful exploration of thinking as an ego function which is to be found in the *Project* – an exploration which, in the latter, even concerns itself with errors in logic! This issue is the only one in the *Project* on which Freud writes a note to himself to go into the matter later in more detail:

They [*the biological rules*] are protected by threats of unpleasure, they are derived from experience, and they can be transposed directly into the rules of logic – which will have to be proved in detail.

(S.E., p. 386)

It seems clear that the analysis of the relationship between the various types of thinking and the origin of errors is by no means finished and the likelihood is that a more sophisticated analysis will be able to integrate them into a still more comprehensive whole. But once again, is it not noteworthy how much further Freud went in analysing these basic mechanisms of thinking in the *Project* than in any later writing?

CONSCIOUS THOUGHT AND THE ROLE OF SPEECH

We are now in a position to discuss how thoughts can achieve conscious-ness by becoming associated with verbal images. In fact the appearance of the first conscious memories displays this integration, since speech arises through cognition:

The biological development of this extremely important [kind of] association also deserves consideration. Speech-innervation is originally a path of discharge for ψ, operating like a safety-valve, . . . it is a portion of the path to *internal change*, which represents the only discharge till the *specific action* has been found. [For all this cf. pp. 317–18.] This path acquires a secondary function from the fact that it draws the attention of the helpful person (usually the wished-for object itself) to the child's longing and distressful state; and thereafter it serves for *communication* and is thus drawn into the specific action. At the start of the function of judgement, when the per-ceptions, on account of their possible connection with their wished-for object, are arousing interest, and their complexes (as has already been shown [pp. 328 and 331–2]) are dissected into an unassimilable component (the thing) and one known to the ego from its own experience (attribute, activity) – what we call *understanding* –, [at this point] two links emerge in relation to utterance by speech. In the first place, there are objects – perceptions – that make one *scream*, because they arouse pain; and it turns out as an immensely important fact that this association of a sound (which arouses motor images of one's own as well) with a perceptual [image], which is composite [*composed*] apart from this, emphasizes that object as a hostile one and serves to direct attention to the perceptual [image]. When otherwise, owing to pain, one has received no good indication of the quality of the object, the *information of one's own scream* serves to characterize the object. Thus this association is a means of making memories that arouse *unpleasure* conscious and objects of attention: the first class of *conscious memories* has been created. Not much is now needed in order to invent speech. There are other objects, which constantly produce certain sounds – in whose perceptual complex, that is, a sound plays a part. In virtue of the trend towards *imitation*, which emerges during judging [p. 333], it is possible to find the information of movement attaching to this sound-image. This class of memories, too, can now become conscious. It now still remains to associate intentional sounds with the perceptions; after that, the memories when the indications of sound-discharge are observed become conscious like perceptions and can be cathected from ψ.

Thus we have found that it is characteristic of the process of *cognitive* thought that during it attention is from the first directed to the indications of thought-discharge, to the indications of speech.

(S.E., pp. 366–7)

Note here the emphasis on 'information of one's own scream' to 'characterize the object'. Further 'there are other objects' in whose perception 'sound plays a part', and that 'it is possible to find the information of movement attaching to this sound image'. This is the same 'information of movement' discussed in Chapter 3 in the section on comparing and judging (pp. 100–2) and in the present chapter as a characteristic of observant thought (p. 115). In Chapter 3, we suggested that the distinction between movement (motor release) and action, which is amply founded in current neurophysiological research (see pp. 103; 106), is a primary-secondary process distinction. In the passage just quoted, the *Project* makes this distinction also: 'It now still remains to associate *intentional* sounds with perceptions.' We should like, therefore, to make explicit the fact that this association of intentional sounds and perceptions can be arbitrary, i.e. take the form of symbols, tokens that represent, stand for, the perception.

Thus, it will be remembered that in the seventh chapter of *The Interpretation of Dreams* one of the major reasons that great importance was attributed to consciousness was that it was stimulable by a whole new set of qualities, the qualities attaching to words, and that this phenomenon plays a vital role in thinking. It must be emphasized that *preconscious* thinking does not proceed with indications of quality and therefore does not have to be connected with verbal images. These indications of quality – obtained from verbal images – are necessary only for thinking to be *conscious*. This same hypothesis is set forth in the *Project*, and again in even greater detail.

Freud's line of reasoning, in reaching the conclusion that for thought to be conscious it must be accompanied by indications of reality and that these indications come from speech associations, cannot be improved upon. It should be noticed that the theory is a 'motor' theory in the sense that it requires a discharge of a motor neuron. But it is a motor theory readily amenable to modification in the direction of action. The arguments are maintained in terms of motor speech mechanisms. It is but a step to invoke motor *images*, which are images of acts, the *consequences* of movements (see above, pp. 103; 106). In this manner the excitation from the consequence of words would initially result in directing attention cathexis towards the words themselves, thus to be replaced by implicit words and their imagined consequences.

The point of departure for the theory is to describe a current of association, whether preconscious or unconscious, to discuss the coming to an end of such a current, and then to suggest that it would be important for the current to continue if possible, because:

Now it is clearly the intention of *observing thought* to become acquainted to the furthest possible extent with the pathways leading from the perception; in this manner, indeed, knowledge of the perceptual object is to be made exhaustive. It will be noted that the method of thought here described leads to *cognition*. For that reason a ψ cathexis is once more required for the mnemic images that are reached, but also a mechanism which will lead that cathexis to the right points. How else are the ψ neurones in the ego to know where the cathexis is to be directed to? A mechanism of attention such as that described above again presupposes, however, indications of quality. Do these arise during the associative passage [of quantity]? Not as a rule, according to our presuppositions. They can, however, be obtained by means of a fresh contrivance of the following description. Indications of quality come about normally only from perceptions; it is thus a question of obtaining a perception from the passage of $Q\dot\eta$. If a discharge were linked to the passage of $Q\dot\eta$ (in addition to the [mere] circulation), then, like every movement, it [the discharge] would furnish information of the movement [p. 318]. After all, indications of quality themselves are only information of discharge [p. 325] (of what kind [we may learn] later perhaps). Now it may happen that during the passage of Q a motor neurone is cathected as well, which then discharges $Q\dot\eta$ and furnishes an indication of quality. It is a question, however, of receiving discharges of this kind from all cathexes. They are not all motor, and for this purpose, therefore, they must be brought into a secure facilitation with motor neurones.

This purpose is fulfilled by *speech association*. This consists in the linking of ψ neurones with neurones which serve sound-presentations and themselves have the closest association with motor speech-*images* [*emphasis ours*]. These associations have an advantage of two characteristics over the others: they are limited (few in number) and exclusive. In any case, from the sound-image the excitation reaches the word-*image* and from it reaches discharge. Thus, if the mnemic *images* are of such a kind that a part-current can go from them to the sound-*images* and motor word-*images*, then the cathexis of the mnemic *images* is accompanied by information of discharge, which is an indication of quality and also accordingly an indication of the consciousness of the memory. If now the ego precathects these word-*images* as it earlier did the images of ω discharge [pp. 360 ff.], then it will have created for itself the mechanism which directs the ψ cathexis to the memories emerging during the passage of $Q\dot{\eta}$. This is *conscious observing thought*.

(S.E., pp. 364–5)

The above passage clearly summarizes the *image* nature of the motor theory. The role of attention is also stated succinctly.

Thus we have found that it is characteristic of the process of *cognitive* thought that during it attention is from the the first directed to the indications of thought-discharge, to the indications of speech. As is well known, indeed, what is called conscious thought takes place to the accompaniment of slight motor expenditure.

(S.E., p. 367)

The intrapsychic (neural as opposed to muscular) nature of thought derived from speech is compared to that of all imaging processes:

... the current of speech-innervations during thought is obviously very small. *We do not really speak, any more than we really move when we imagine a motor image* [*italics ours*].

(S.E., p. 367)

We have already discussed how the existence of a way of representing external events brings with it the danger of mistaking the awakening of a memory from within for a perception from without and thus confusing external and internal reality. The *Project* carries this question a step further by pointing to the danger that currents of association starting from within may bring about changes which can be confused with changes in psychic representations which are the result of real experiences engendered from without. Freud argued that indications of reality – paradoxically by giving thought a kind of *thought* reality, which is to be distinguished from *external* reality – make it possible to

124

remember thoughts and thus to distinguish changes brought about by thinking from changes brought about by external experiences:

As we know, the facilitations between the ψ neurones constitute '*memory*', the representation of all the influences which ψ has experienced from the external world. Now we observe that the ego itself puts in hand cathexes of the ψ neurones as well, and sets going passages [of quantity] which must certainly also leave facilitations behind them as traces. ψ, however, has no means of distinguishing these results of thought-processes from the results of perceptual processes. It may perhaps be possible to cognize and reproduce perceptual processes by their association with ω discharges; but all that remains of the facilitations made by thought is the outcome, not a *memory*. The same thought-facilitation may have come about owing to one intense process or ten less forcible ones. The *indications of speech-discharge* help, however, to make good this lack; they put thought-processes on a level with perceptual processes, lend them reality and *make memory of them possible*. [Cf. p. 335, but also p. 378 below.]

(S.E., pp. 365–6)

And later:

Indications of discharge through speech are also in a certain sense indications of reality but of thought-reality not of external reality. . . .

(S.E., p. 373)

The *Project* thus emphasizes that the 'traces in the form of facilitations' resulting from thinking do occur and that this process applies to pre-conscious as well as conscious thinking:

On the other hand, it is undeniable that thought about a topic leaves extra-ordinarily important traces behind for any subsequent re-thinking about it [cf. pp. 300 and 335]; and it is very questionable whether this is brought about only by thought accompanied by indications of quality and conscious-ness. There must therefore be thought-facilitations. . . .

(S.E., p 379)

A neurological problem is posed by the distinction between facilitations resulting from thinking and those resulting from reality experiences. This problem is handled as follows:

Yet it must be possible to find a means of reconciling and explaining [*this distinction*] in the fact that thought-facilitations were all first created at a high level [*of side-cathexes*] and that they probably also come into effect at a high level once more, whereas associative facilitations, which originated during full or primary passage [of quantity], re-appear when conditions for an unbound passage [of quantity] are established.

(S.E., p. 379)

Freud admitted that, none the less, the possibility of confusing thought and reality facilitations remained:

Accordingly, then, some possible effect by thought-facilitations upon associative facilitations is not to be denied.

(S.E., p. 379)

Thus thought facilitations and associative facilitations distinguish two varieties of memory organization. Rapaport (1951) conceived of them as the distinction between conceptual and drive organizations of memory. In our Chapter 1, and in the *Project*, they are set forth as a cognitive constructional as contrasted to a purely associational (neuron-to-neuron discharge) organization.

The adaptive value accruing from the fact that thinking can become conscious is especially stressed in the *Project*. We noted earlier (p. 119) some incomplete statements concerning the rule of attention as it applied to thinking in our discussion of the fact that this 'rule' is the basis for 'logic'. In fact, the very existence of preconscious thinking is a result of the fact that thinking does *not* automatically result in indications of quality, or reality. We now note that the rule does not apply to preconscious thinking, since in such thinking there are no indications of reality, but it does apply to conscious thinking, since in such thinking there *are* indications of reality:

. . . it must be emphasized that the biological rule of attention stated above is abstracted from perception [p. 371] and applies in the first instance only to indications of reality. Indications of discharge through speech are also in a certain sense indications of reality – but of thought-reality not of external reality, and in their case a rule of this kind has not by any means come into effect, because no constant threat of unpleasure would be attached to a breach of it. The unpleasure through neglecting cognition is not so glaring as that from ignoring the external world, though at bottom they are one and the same.

(S.E., pp. 372–3)

The circular character of the feedback mechanism operating in the directing of attention in thinking is expressed – not too clearly – in the view that not only do indications of thought reality lead to the directing of attention but also the direction of attention to thinking leads to indications of thought reality:

In view of the undoubted utility of arousing the indications [*consciousness*] of thought, we may expect to find contrivances to ensure their arousal. Indications of thought are not, indeed, generated spontaneously like indications of reality, without the participation of ψ. Here observation tells us that these contrivances do not apply for all cases of thought-process as they do for investigating thought. The necessary condition for indications of thought being aroused at all is, of course, their being cathected by attention; they come about in that case in virtue of the law that, when two neurones are linked and simultaneously cathected, conduction [between them] is favoured [p. 319].

(S.E., p. 374)

The principal point of the adaptive utility of consciousness is that it provides a mechanism that can be pitted against that by which thought may be influenced by purposive cathexis. In short, only by conscious, attentive thought can the organism be protected against 'wishful thinking'.

. . . attention to the indications of quality ensures the impartiality of the passage [of association]. For it is very difficult for the ego to put itself into the situation of mere '*investigation*'. The ego almost always has purposive or wishful cathexes, whose presence during investigation, as we shall see [p. 376], influences the passage of association and so produces a false knowledge of perceptions. Now there is no better protection against this falsification of thought than if an ordinarily displaceable $Q\dot{\eta}$ is directed to [? by] the ego to a region which cannot manifest a diversion such as this. . . . There is only a single such expedient – if, namely, attention is directed to the indications of quality, [*indications*] which are not [*of*] purposive ideas, . . .

Thus thought accompanied by cathexis of the indications of thought-reality or of the indications of speech is the highest, securest form of cognitive thought-process.

(S.E., pp. 373–4)

But the *Project* recognizes that the goal is an ideal that is often not reached:

Yet the *attraction* produced by the precathexis of the indications of thought has only a certain degree of force in fighting against other influences. Thus, for instance, every other cathexis in the neighbourhood of the passage [of association] (purposive cathexes, affective cathexes) will compete with it and make the passage [of association] unconscious.

(S.E., p. 374)

In summary, we have outlined the manner in which the *Project* delineates *speech as essential to permit thoughts to become conscious*, and to permit a better differentiation between thought and reality facilitations and thus to allow thought to proceed unimpeded by purposive cathexes in so far as possible. Is not this, then, the initial rationale for the role of insight in therapy – with speech essential to permit thoughts to become conscious? Freud continued to believe that words play a vital role in thinking and as speech in bringing thought to consciousness and therefore in influencing conduct. This belief was maintained through all the rest of his theorizing, despite the fact that he granted that some kinds of thinking could take place by way of visual images. He especially stressed that thinking which involved the *relationships* between ideas had to take place by way of words and that speech was the vehicle for making these relationships conscious. (See Gill, 1963.)

THE RELATIONSHIP BETWEEN
PRIMARY AND SECONDARY PROCESSES

As we have seen (pp. 82–3), the model in the *Project* includes the genetic description of how the secondary processes are elaborated from the primary processes, and that the terms 'taming' and 'signal', which are the catchwords which label this genetic development, are already present in the *Project*. However, primary processes do not become extinct and can under certain circumstances dominate the course of neural function. Their principal mode of eruption is in affect, and this is the reason that in the *Project* there is often a close connection between affect and the primary process. We already noted the way

. . . the generation of affect inhibits the normal passage of thought. . . . This happens firstly, in that many paths of thought are forgotten which would ordinarily come into account – similarly, that is, to what occurs in dreams [p. 338]. . . . The recent pathway succumbed in the affective state . . . that is, what was *old-established* . . . gained the upper hand. . . . Secondly, [affect inhibits thought] in that without forgetting, pathways are followed which are ordinarily avoided: in particular, pathways leading to discharge, [such as] actions [performed] in the affect[ive state]. In conclusion, the affective process approximates to the uninhibited primary process.

(S.E., p. 357)

Of course, the *Project* also describes secondary process affect under the 'signal' concept which we discussed above (p. 120). Thus, in general, affective processes are local, but they can become widespread when there are large quantities of excitation with which to deal. In such instances, there is the likelihood of a primary 'passions' process as opposed to a secondary 'reasons' process. This explanation is provided in the *Project*, as noted in the section on errors in thinking (p. 119) when affect swamps the system.

Let us review once more the manner in which memories capable of generating affect are 'tamed' until the affect provides only a 'signal'. We do this in anticipation of the problem to be discussed next: what determines whether a primary or secondary process will control behaviour:

What is it, then, that happens to *memories* capable of affect till they are *tamed*? . . . these memories with their capacity for affect [?] Being traces of experiences of pain, they have been cathected (according to our hypothesis about pain [p. 307]) with excessively large $Q\phi$ and have acquired an excessively strong facilitation to the release of unpleasure and affect. Particularly large and repeated binding from the ego is required before this facilitation to unpleasure can be counterbalanced.

(S.E., pp. 380–81)

And for the signal concept:

. . . the release of unpleasure was quantitatively restricted, and its start was precisely a signal for the ego to set normal defence in action [p. 326]; this guarded against fresh experiences of pain, with their facilitations, developing so easily.

(S.E., p. 358)

And further:

. . . with a release of unpleasure, . . . simultaneously the ego is at work, too, creating side-cathexes. . . . the release [of unpleasure] is less the second time, until, after further repetition, it shrivels up to the intensity of a signal acceptable to the ego [cf. p. 326 above].

(S.E., p. 359)

There is thus a tendency to conservation which goes beyond simple inertia and motor discharge: certain short-cuts to discharge are not taken because the organism has, in addition to the propensity to simple discharge, the propensity to develop habits (memory facilitations) for particular *forms* of discharge that it stays with, even though these represent longer and more delayed paths than the short-cuts would be.

In this fashion, the question of the relationship between primary and secondary processes is raised in the *Project* on a concrete level whenever there is a discussion of behaviour, i.e. whether or not a particular action is a retracing simply of motor facilitation or whether the more complex constructive 'reality' search is made by the brain for 'identity' between wishful cathexis and external object.

These issues are as difficult and alive today as they were in 1895. In a section entitled 'Primary and Secondary Processes Reconsidered', Neisser concludes:

It is fair to say that no contemporary psychological theory and no existing program deals satisfactorily with the constructive nature of the higher mental processes. This deficiency will not be remedied here. As noted earlier, a serious theory of memory and thinking is beyond the scope of this book. I can, however, suggest an analogy which may be helpful. Like the Gestalt psychologists, though for different reasons, I believe that the processes of *visual cognition,* and perception in general, may serve as useful models for memory and thought. . . .

I am proposing . . . a two-stage mechanism [of thinking], analogous to those of vision and hearing. First, the so-called primary processes make an array of crudely defined 'objects' or 'ideas,' along lines which tend to follow the structure of the 'input,' i.e., the information in memory. Then, in alert and waking subjects, the secondary processes of directed thought select among these objects and develop them further. In this interpretation, the primary and secondary processes are by no means as antagonistic as Freud believed. One is essential to the other. Rational thought is 'secondary' in the sense that it works with objects already formed by a 'primary' process. If these objects receive no secondary elaboration, as in some dreams and dis-organized mental states, we experience them in the fleeting and imprecise way that characterizes the uncoded figures of iconic memory. However, the same multiple processes that produce these shadowy and impalpable experi-ences are also essential preliminaries to directed thinking.

The notion that the secondary process can serve to elaborate primary-process material is an old one. It has often been advanced in connection with the problem of 'creativity' (e.g., Kris, 1950; Maslow, 1957). However, the present suggestion goes further. It seems to me that *all* directed thinking is an elaboration of this sort, just as *all* visual and auditory perception depends on prior wholistic construction of some kind of unit.

Also familiar is the idea that the primary process, as defined by Freud, has a perceptual function; it is often said to manifest itself in such phenomena as 'subliminal perception' and 'perceptual defense.' Some have even supposed that the primary processes comprise a separate cognitive system with super-sensitive capacities, able to detect and react to stimuli that are otherwise subthreshold. This hypothesis must be rejected; in previous chapters, we have repeatedly found contaminating artifacts in the experiments which seem to support it. I am making a different suggestion. There is indeed a stage of perception which corresponds to the primary processes of thought, but the relation between them is one of functional similarity, not identity. In remem-bering and thinking, as in perception, the secondary process further examines and further develops the objects made available to it by the primary one.

(Neisser, 1967, pp. 300–303)

Perusal of the *Project* as we have done here shows that Freud did in fact conceive of secondary process thinking as an elaboration of primary processes. In contrast to Neisser, however, Freud uses the same neurological mechanism to accomplish secondary process per-ception, action and thinking. Thinking is retracing the same paths, constructing the same structures, but with 'smaller quantities', less expenditure of energy or effort – less work, less motor discharge. In the *Project* thought is considered as implicit perception and action, a conception akin to that proposed by Bartlett (1958) who, however, fails to develop concepts regarding the structure of the thought process.

The question is thus raised as to when a primary rather than a secondary process becomes manifest and when perception and specific willed actions occur rather than, or in addition to, thought. The factors responsible deal with the expenditures of energy and effort involved in overcoming the resistances (at synapses) that maintain effective or ineffective and efficient or inefficient modes of behaviour.

But we have now come to the difficult area of the operation of primary associative and dissociative processes, an area about which the *Project* contains a great deal of analysis crucial to any coherent understanding of pathological psychological phenomena. The final chapter will essay an introduction to this field of problems.

[5]

DREAMS AND PSYCHOPATHOLOGY: ASSOCIATIVE AND DISSOCIATIVE PROCESSES

A BRIEF REVIEW AND PREVIEW

We now turn to that area of psychological mechanisms, the primary associative and dissociative processes, which in ordinary life is shrouded behind a scaffolding of secondary cognitive structures. Our purpose is to show that the *Project* contains the essential descriptions of primary processes as they appear in dreams and psychopathology; that for the most part, even in these states, a compromise between primary and secondary processes is manifest; and that a number of basic tenets not only of the metapsychology but of psychoanalytic clinical theory are already clearly described.

Let us recall from Chapter 1, and some of the succeeding discussions on the differences between primary and secondary processes, the issues central to the distinction. These may be profitably reviewed once more now that we have the entire panorama of secondary processes at our disposal. In a somewhat simplified version, the following outlines can be drawn.

The essence of the neurological structure of the ψ system is the fact that multiple alternative paths are available through it to make potential associative connections between external exigencies, endogenous chemistry and the organism's movements. The variety of these alternative potential pathways is, however, limited by two sets of feedback mechanisms which constrain the behaviour of the organism: 'attentional' that initially regulate responses to external exigencies, and 'drive' that initially regulate responses to endogenous chemistry.

These two types of feedback constrain the variety of potential alternative paths to the development of some against the rest – developments which become the memory-motive structure of facilitated pathways. In essence, these are the associative structures of wishes which, unless inhibited, would tend to malfunction whenever there exists an imbalance between internal and external stimulation.

Inhibition is furnished, however, by an executive ego process derived as a defence against this malfunctioning by further constraining the mechanism of the drives. As feedbacks, the drive mechanisms can either be negative and equilibratory or positive and disruptive. Disruption is defended against by an inhibitory mechanism that tilts the functioning of the memory-motive facilitations in the direction of perception and willed action rather than peremptory discharges leading to wishful hallucination and impulsive movement. The inhibitory mechanism, in combination with the facilitatory, becomes an information processing, cognitive feedforward operation.

In the *Project* facilitation and inhibition are meshed by the hypothesis of lateral or side-cathexes assumed to operate orthogonal to facilitations. Side-cathexes are thus thought to bind excitation and prevent peremptory discharge through the facilitated pathways. Contemporary neurophysiology has made little of such side-cathexes but has identified a separate inhibitory system that operates by way of synaptic hyperpolarization (see Ch. 3) to act as an executive processor to the brain.

Whenever the inhibitory executive defences become inoperative, the primary associative and facilitatory memory-motive structures with their 'error processing' feedback mechanisms (recall Ch. 1) become manifest. This occurs for a variety of reasons in sleep where it produces dreams, and in psychopathology as we will shortly see. Since two types of feedback exist, attentional and drive, two types of primary process can be identified: those related to attention and reality testing such as hallucination and projection; and those related to drive and drive restraint such as compulsion and repression. For the most part, these symptom formations involve compromise formations, which are complex mixtures of primary and secondary processes that lead to dissociation in the sense that they often result in a skewing of the executive functions of the ego in 'favour' of one memory-motive structure at the sacrifice of integrating the entire range of such structures. The descriptions in the *Project* of these compromise mechanisms form an able preface to subsequent psychoanalytic clinical theory.

SLEEP AND DREAMS

Despite the fact that the editors of the *Project* believe that the attempt at a theory of dreams is fragmentary in so many essential portions that it doesn't seem worthwhile to compare it in detail with *The Interpretation of Dreams*, we believe the crux of Freud's theories of sleep and dreams is to be found in the *Project* and that an analysis of the *Project* from this point of view sheds valuable light on the development of Freud's thinking.

We propose that the centering of Freud's model on dreams, as was done in *The Interpretation of Dreams*, tended to misplace the proper emphasis of the model, with an underemphasis of secondary processes, rectified later when Freud proposed the structural theory. Indeed a remark in a letter from Freud to Fliess suggests that Freud was aware that his presentation of the model in the seventh chapter of *The Interpretation of Dreams* was skewed by the fact that it was written in the context of the book about dreams. Freud wrote (Letter 90, 9th June 1898): 'It is abominably difficult to set out the new psychology in so far as it relates to dreams, as it is necessarily fragmentary only . . .' (*Origins*, p. 255). It has been said (Bertram Lewin, 1955) that psychoanalysis can be conceived from the point of view of dreams or of psychopathology; that Freud chose the dream as the focal point in the seventh chapter; that he then turned to psychopathology as the focus; and that the two need to be better integrated. It is also known that a very interesting chapter in Freud's development lies in his several times recognizing and forgetting the fact that dreams and symptoms are built along the same lines.

Freud twice in the *Project* states the similarity between dreams and symptoms:

A second fact of the same importance is that the pathological mechanisms which are revealed in the psychoneuroses by the most careful analysis have the greatest similarity to dream-processes. The most important conclusions follow from this comparison, which will be enlarged on later [p. 341].

(S.E., p. 336)

And:

If, when the memory of a dream is retained, we enquire into its content, we find that the meaning of dreams as wish-fulfilments is concealed by a number of ψ processes; all of which are met with once more in neuroses and characterize the latter's pathological nature [p. 336].

(S.E., p. 341)

We will soon return to this passage in another connection.

We suggest that neither dreams nor symptoms should be the focal point of an exposition of the model. They are applications of the model to the understanding of dreams and symptoms. These latter two have come to occupy the role they have in clinical discussion because analysis is so strongly related to psychopathology, because the model of the seventh chapter was written under the influence of the discovery of infantile sexuality – and hence focused on the drives rather than external reality – and because only in dreams and pathology can one see with any clarity the primary processes which are generally the hidden side of the double-sided apparatus functioning in a complex interplay of primary and secondary processes. We agree with Hartmann (1958) and Rapaport (1960) that the model is a general psychological model, and we further believe that its most balanced presentation is as Freud presented it in the *Project*.

Before discussing dreams themselves we must deal with the nature of sleep as it appears in the *Project*. The primary and secondary *functions* of the nervous system (S.E., pp. 335–6) are reviewed succinctly and the point is made that sleep and dreams are a museum piece of antiquity which shed such strong light on the development of the psychic apparatus. The condition which makes sleep possible is:

. . . a *lowering of the endogenous load in the ψ nucleus,* which makes the secondary function superfluous.

(S.E., p. 336)

This is related to infants sleeping as long as they are undisturbed by physical needs or external stimuli. (Note that both internal and external stimuli are stressed and that the condition of sleep drastically reduces the energy requirements of the system.)

In adults this store [*of excitation derived from exogenous and endogenous stimulation*] is collected in the 'ego' [p. 323]; we may assume that it is the *unloading of the ego* which determines and characterizes sleep. And here, as is immediately clear, we have the *precondition of psychical primary processes*.

(S.E., p. 336)

So it is the lowering of the 'load' (by adjustments of endogenous and exogenous inputs to the primary feedback processes) on the ego which permits sleep, a condition in which the secondary (information) processes are unnecessary and primary processes are unveiled.

As noted in Chapter 1, the *Project* described sleep as characterized by '*motor paralysis (paralysis of the will)*' (S.E., p. 337) and states that

Dreams *are devoid of motor discharge* and, for the most part, of motor elements. We are paralysed in dreams [p. 337].

(S.E., p. 338)

Sleep is also characterized by a cessation of external perception; since ψ withdraws

these pallium cathexes, the perceptions take place upon uncathected neurones and are slight, and perhaps not capable of giving an indication of quality from ω [p. 325].

(S.E., p. 337)

And thus the hallucinatory nature of dreams 'is the most important characteristic of sleep' (S.E., p. 339).

The remark in the *Project* about the insusceptibility to excitation of uncathected systems, in connection with perception in sleep, makes one realize the close relationship between the two primary laws – the law of reflex attention and the law of reflex defence.

Thus, by an automatic mechanism, the counterpart of the mechanism of attention, ψ excludes the ϕ impressions so long as it itself is uncathected.

(S.E., p. 337)

Is not defence designed to prevent a particular content from being susceptible to excitation by removing its cathexis as completely as possible? And is then the principle of the unexcitability of an uncathected system not the same as the law of defence?

In the same vein, discussion of dreams is introduced by a question the relevance of which is not at first clear. Freud asks whether *primary* ψ processes can take place without the cathexis of attention. He suggests that clues to its answer lie in the fact that sleep is disturbed by cathexes entering ψ from ϕ.

This seems to indicate that during day-time a constant, even though displaceable, cathexis (*attention*) is sent into the pallium neurones, which receive perception from ϕ [p. 315], so that it may well be that the carrying-out of the ψ primary processes [*in dreams*] is made possible with the help of this ψ contribution [p. 336].

(S.E., p. 337)

Thus dreams are introduced by the question of how *attention* differs in the absence of a contribution from ϕ, i.e. from the external world. This question leads to the definition of dreams in terms of primary ψ processes and their wish-fulfilling nature. We believe, therefore, that this line of reasoning is an early but incomplete attempt in the *Project* to delineate an essential distinction between manifest and latent dreams and how the former (manifest) is a distortion of the latter (latent) by way of the mechanisms of attention and defence. For the contribution of attention and defence to the dream-as-a-primary-ψ-process is the contribution of secondary ego processes. The *Project* has a partial insight into this issue. For example:

It is not certain whether in adults the *ego* is completely relieved of its burden in sleep. In any case it withdraws an enormous number of its cathexes, which, however, are restored on awakening, immediately and without trouble.

(S.E., p. 336)

And:

If the ego were completely unloaded, sleep would necessarily be dreamless.

(S.E., p. 339)

The wish-fulfilling function of dreams was, as has already been noted in passing, clearly enunciated in the *Project*:

They [dreams] are *wish-fulfilments* – that is, primary processes following upon experiences of satisfaction [p. 319] . . .

(S.E., p. 340)

While it is generally believed that Freud's theory of the wish-fulfilling function of dreams is an inductive conclusion based on the empirical analysis of many dreams, and while it is true that empirical analysis has confirmed the wish-fulfilment theory, there is good evidence that the theory was at least as much an inevitable deduction following from the model Freud had constructed. This point is well made in a recent paper by Raymond Fancher (1971). A telling quotation from *The Interpretation of Dreams*, pointing in the direction of this conclusion, is this: 'Thought is after all nothing but a substitute for a hallucinatory wish; and *it is self-evident that dreams must be wish-fulfilments, since nothing but a wish can set our mental apparatus at work*' (emphasis added; *The Interpretation of Dreams*, S.E., vol. 5, p. 567).

But it was the inadequate understanding of the role of the ego in dreams – despite Freud's recognition of the relationship between dreams and symptoms as well as his recognition that 'dreams exhibit every [*degree of*] transition to the waking state and . . . [*of ad*] mixture with normal ψ processes' (S.E., p. 338) – which was responsible for the following inadequacies of Freud's theory of dreams in the *Project*, as compared with his discussion in *The Interpretation of Dreams*.

1) Freud suggested that it is difficult to recognized reams as wish-fulfilments:

because the release of pleasure (the reproduction of traces of pleasurable discharges [p. 312]) in them is slight, because in general they run their course almost without affect (without motor release).

(S.E., p. 340)

The same idea was expressed in a transitional formulation in *The Interpretation of Dreams*, but Freud recognized there that the real reason affect seems slight in dreams is because of inhibition by censorship:

. . . it may be that the centrifugal calling-up of affects by unconscious thinking may become more difficult during sleep. In that case the affective impulses occurring during the course of the dream-thoughts would from their very nature be weak impulses, and consequently those which found their way into the dream would be no less weak. On this view, then, the 'suppression of affect' would not in any way be the consequence of the dream-work but would result from the state of sleep. This may be true, but it cannot be the whole truth. . . . We shall by and large scarcely be wrong if we regard the suppression of affect as a consequence of the inhibition which these contraries [*every train of thought is yoked with its contradictory opposite and all these trains of thought are capable of carrying an affect*] exercise upon each other and which the censorship exercises upon the impulsions suppressed by it. The *inhibition of affect, accordingly, must be considered as a second consequence of the censorship of dreams, just as dream-distortion is its first consequence.*

(S.E., vol. 5, p. 468)

2) This failure to emphasize the function of defence in transforming the latent into the manifest dream and therefore the concentration on the latent dream led Freud to write:

The connections in dreams are partly *nonsensical*, partly *feeble-minded*, or even meaningless or strangely crazy.

(S.E., p. 338)

But he did recognize what is now described as secondary revision of this 'compulsion to associate'.

3) The same reason, i.e. the failure to emphasize the function of ego defences in dreams, led Freud to conclude that the 'nonsensical, partly feeble-minded' appearance of dreams

. . . show[s] that a part of the [dreamer's] psychical experiences have been forgotten. Actually, indeed, all the biological experiences which ordinarily inhibit the primary process are forgotten, and this is owing to the lack of ego-cathexis. The senselessness and illogicality of dreams are probably to be attributed to this very same characteristic.

(S.E., p. 338)

He also wrote:

It is noteworthy how poorly dreams are remembered . . .   (S.E., p. 340)

Later through the study of the relations between manifest and latent dreams Freud came to the conclusion that there is a hypermnesia in dreams, but to understand that he had to recognize the role played in dreams by inhibition, by censorship.

4) Freud wrote that dreams do 'little harm . . . compared with other primary processes' (S.E., p. 340):

But this is easily explained from the fact that, for the most part, they follow old facilitations and thus make no change [in them], that ϕ experiences are held back from them and that, owing to the paralysis of motility, they [dreams] do not leave traces of discharge behind them.
                                                          (S.E., p. 340)

But there are those who believe that dreams can sometimes have a very powerful influence on waking life and may even precipitate psychoses. The role that the ego *does* play in dreams may be some evidence on the side of those who believe that dreams can to some extent initiate rather than merely reflect a pathological process.

5) Freud's puzzlement as to what determines what becomes conscious in a dream is again a reflection of his incomplete understanding of the manifest dream. He knew something was missing in his reasoning and he came close to the answer when he wrote:

What happens is not, for instance, that the wish becomes conscious and that its fulfilment is then hallucinated, but only the latter: the intermediate link is left to be inferred. It has quite certainly been passed through, but without being able to develop qualitatively. It is evident, however, that the cathexis of the wishful idea cannot possibly be stronger than the motive impelling to it. Thus the psychical passage [of excitation] in dreams takes place in accordance with Q; but it is not Q which decides the question of becoming conscious.

                                                          (S.E., p. 342)

It is important to note that Freud was perfectly clear in the *Project* that consciousness can attach to primary processes as well as to secondary, as we noted in the earlier section on consciousness (p. 20):

. . . *consciousness* in dreams furnishes quality with as little trouble as in waking life. This shows that consciousness does not cling to the ego but can become an addition to any ψ processes. It warns us, too, against possibly identifying primary processes with unconscious ones.
                                                          (S.E., p. 340)

Here is the kernel of the failure of the psychoanalytic theory of 'topographic' systems, of course. Conscious processes are not necessarily higher in the psychic hierarchy than preconscious processes (see Gill, 1963). But the *Project* does make a vital distinction between consciousness of primary and of secondary processes:

Consciousness of dream ideas is above all discontinuous. What becomes conscious is not a whole succession of associations, but only separate stopping points in it. Between these there lie unconscious intermediate links which we can easily discover when we are awake.

(S.E., p. 341)

Which 'stopping points' become 'conscious' and which become 'unconscious intermediaries' depend on the amount of cathexis available to each and this in turn depends entirely on the principle of association by simultaneity (Ch. 2): 'This now became conscious . . . owing to pressure from both sides' (S.E., p. 342). Thus mechanisms such as displacement and condensation characterize the primary dream process:

It is very puzzling that . . . the intermediate link . . . [*does not become*] conscious as well, and an explanation of this is called for. . . . The puzzle about unconscious intermediate links applies equally to waking thought, where similar events are of daily occurrence. But what remains characteristic of dreams is the *ease with which Qη is displaced* [in them] [*added emphasis ours*].

(S.E., p. 342)

Again:

If a perception comes from ϕ in waking life, it is no doubt made *clearer* by ψ cathexis (interest) but *not more vivid*; it does not alter its quantitative characteristic [*emphasis ours*].

(S.E., pp. 339–40)

These same points are expressed thus in *The Interpretation of Dreams*:

In normal mental life, too, we find ideas which, being the nodal points or end-results of whole chains of thought, possess a high degree of psychical significance; but their significance is not expressed by any feature that is obvious in a *sensory* manner to internal perception; their perceptual presentation is not in any respect more intense on account of their psychical significance. In the process of condensation, on the other hand, every psychical interconnection is transformed into an *intensification* of its ideational content.

(S.E., vol. 5, p. 595)

The main theses of the model of sleep and dream formation are present, then, in the *Project* – the cathectic changes in sleep; the paralysis of motility and the cessation of external perception in sleep; the dream as a survival in the normal mind of primary process functioning; dream as wishfulfilment; concealment of the wish; topographic regression; the similarity between dream and symptom formation; displacement and condensation, though the latter not yet named – but what was missing, aside, of course, from the discovery of infantile sexuality as content, was a clear recognition of the role of the ego, of the defences. Freud had not clearly seen that the dream is a *compromise* formation. This lack of clarity is shown by his asking whether attention cathexis necessarily plays a role in primary ψ processes. We shall see another variant of the same unclarity in our next section on another illustration of the model, i.e. symptom formation. It is expressed there by asking how a primary process can take place in the presence of a functioning ego. And it is answered by the curious hypothesis which resulted from the combined effect of lack of clarity about dream and symptom formation as compromises, and the fact that infantile sexuality had not yet been discovered – the hypothesis of 'posthumous' primary processes.

SYMPTOM FORMATION

Central to the problem of understanding the operation of primary processes in psychopathology is the fact of their occurrence in the presence of a functioning ego. Once it is capable of registering representations of the external world, the psychological apparatus acquires the even more extraordinary capacity of being able to manipulate these representations so that it can experimentally study action in the external world without actually undertaking such action. But together with these capacities for registering external experience and experimentally manipulating it, the psychic apparatus – in an organism like man at any rate – acquires a nearly fatal flaw. It runs the risk of confusing a representation of the external world awakened from within with the actual presence of the object in the external world. In short, it becomes subject to hallucination, that is, the inability to distinguish an internally aroused image from the perception of an object.

So thoroughly ingrained is this defect that it is in fact the primary way in which the apparatus works: hallucination is in a sense *the* mechanism of the primary process:

... the primary memory of a perception is always a hallucination ...

(S.E., p. 339)

And:

... *primary wishful cathexis, too, was of a hallucinatory nature* [p. 319].

(S.E., p. 340)

And:

I do not doubt that in the first instance this wishful activation will produce the same thing as a perception – namely a *hallucination*.

(S.E., p. 319)

As we noted earlier (p. 75), the very essence of the result of the primary process is hallucination:

Wishful cathexis to the point of hallucination [and] complete generation of unpleasure which involves a complete expenditure of defence are described by us as *psychical primary processes*. . . .

(S.E., pp. 326–7)

The organism requires a means of distinguishing between an image and a percept and Freud finds such means in what he calls 'an indication of quality'. It will be recalled that in discussing quantity and quality in the functioning of the nervous system we emphasized that quality is derivable only from externally derived perception and from memory derived pleasure and unpleasure. When there is an indication of quality the organism comes to construe the experience as a percept, not a hallucination, since the indication of qualities derived from the external world are by far the more frequent:

For the difference is that the *indication of quality* follows, if it comes from outside, whatever the intensity of the cathexis, whereas, if it comes from ψ, it does so only when there are large intensities. It is accordingly *inhibition by the ego which makes possible a criterion for distinguishing between perception and memory.*

(S.E., p. 326)

And only:

If the wished-for object is abundantly cathected, so that it is activated in a hallucinatory manner, the same indication of discharge or of reality follow[s] . . . as in the case of external perception.

(S.E., p. 325)

It is in fact the necessity for limiting the amount of quantity of the wishful cathexis, that is, to prevent a hallucination, which leads to the inhibition of the primary process by the secondary process:

It learns further that it must not cathect the wishful idea beyond a certain amount since otherwise it would deceive itself in a hallucinatory manner [pp. 325–6].

(S.E., p. 369)

And:

The fact that a memory exhibits a hallucinatory characteristic for so long also calls for an explanation – important for our view of hallucination. Here it is plausible to suppose that this capacity for hallucination, as well as the capacity for affect, are indications of the fact that the ego-cathexis [*inhibition*] has not yet gained any influence on the memory [*facilitation*], that the primary lines of discharge [*the memory-motive structure*] and the full or primary process [*associative, chemical or motor discharge*] predominate in it.

(S.E., p. 381)

One of the results of this grave flaw in the psychological apparatus is 'projection', the attributing of one's feelings to others, adopted because the organism has a better shield against external stimuli than against endogenous ones and so is better able to deal with an external than an internal stimulus. This is most clearly stated in *Beyond the Pleasure Principle* (1920):

. . . a particular way is adopted by dealing with any internal excitations which produce too great an increase of unpleasure: there is a tendency to treat them as though they were acting, not from the inside, but from the outside, so that it may be possible to bring the shield against stimuli into operation as a means of defence against them. This is the origin of *projection*, which is destined to play such a large part in the causation of pathological processes.

(S.E., vol. 18, p. 29)

Another reason that an external stimulus can be better dealt with than an internal one is that an external one can be escaped from by a movement, whereas the constant pressure of an endogenous stimulus or memory can be escaped from only by the effort and work involved in constructing a 'specific action'. As expressed in the *Project*:

. . . among the paths of discharge those are preferred and retained which involve a cessation of the stimulus: *flight from the stimulus* . . . there is a proportion between the Q of excitation and the effort necessary for the flight from the stimulus, so that the principle of *inertia* is not upset by this.

(S.E., p. 296)

The same point is made in later writings and then the fact that some stimuli disappear on flight and others do not is itself made the basis for distinguishing between outer and inner, that is, is regarded as a means of reality testing:

On the one hand, it [*the organism*] will be aware of stimuli which can be avoided by muscular action (flight); these it ascribes to an external world. On the other hand, it will also be aware of stimuli against which such action is of no avail. . . . The perceptual substance of the living organism will thus have found in the efficacy of its muscular activity a basis for distinguishing between an 'outside' and 'inside'.

(*Instincts and their Vicissitudes*, 1915, S.E., vol. 14, p. 119)

And:

The antithesis ego–non-ego (external), i.e., subject–object, is . . . thrust upon the individual organism at an early stage, by the experience that it can silence *external* stimuli by means of muscular action but is defenceless against *instinctual* [*should read* drive *since the original is 'Triebe'*] stimuli.

(ibid., p. 134)

The discussion of the mechanisms involved in primary processes that occur during symptom formation begins, as did the *Project* as a whole, with a consideration about quantity, for Freud's clinical point of departure is compulsive, '*excessively intense* ideas' (S.E., p. 347); as we recall, he had in fact written at the outset of the *Project* that:

[*The quantitative conception*] is derived directly from pathological clinical observation especially where excessively intense ideas were concerned . . .

(S.E., p. 295)

Here an inordinate increase in load, in the amount of energy and effort, is involved, in contrast to the sleep state where load is sharply decreased. Note, however, that in keeping with the tenets of control theory, in both sleep and symptom formation, primary processes become manifest when marked changes in load (or in today's clinical languages, stress) occur.

Freud follows what was a central pattern for his exposition and understanding of pathological phenomena – their comparison and contrast with related normal phenomena. In this instance he compared normal and abnormal compulsions – excessively intense ideas, the abnormal being incomprehensible, incongruous, and incapable of being cleared up by any process of thought; while the normal are comprehensible, congruous and 'in healthy people a compulsion such as this persists for only a short time after its occasion, and gradually disintegrates' (S.E., p. 348). This last point may be compared with the suggestion that facilitations which are not used gradually disappear.

But the absurdity and incongruity of symptoms are more clearly recognized as a result of distortion than are the '*nonsensical*, . . . even meaningless, strangely crazy' (S.E., p. 338) dreams, for:

In analysis we learn, too, the process by which the appearance of absurdity and *incongruity* comes about.

(S.E., p. 348)

It is in the same connection that the *Project* proposes the now classical view that insight is the essentially mutative factor in analysis:

Now our analyses show that a hysterical compulsion is *resolved* immediately it is *explained* (made intelligible).

(S.E., p. 348)

The primary 'compulsive' process which Freud particularly stressed in the *Project* is displacement, though, as we shall see shortly (p. 146), there is an indication of 'isolation', described as 'repression *without* symbolization' – symbol meaning substitute, a term which also appears in the *Project*.

In the abnormal symbol, the symbol has completely taken the place of the thing it symbolizes, whereas this is not true of the normal symbol (S.E., p. 349). The symbol is thus an excessively intense substitution, or in current terminology, it has become invested with drive cathexis.

In the *Project* the occasion for primary compulsive processes in psychopathology is conflict, as is also stated in the *Studies on Hysteria* of the same date. The quantity of distress (unpleasure) alone is not responsible for compulsion and repression:

Experience shows, however, that the most distressing memories, which must necessarily arouse the greatest unpleasure (*the memory of remorse over bad actions*) [*emphasis added*] cannot be repressed and replaced by symbols.

(S.E., p. 352)

Part Two of the *Project* describes conflict in terms of a bad conscience related to a case report of an experience which had been repressed:

She now reproached herself for having gone there the second time [*back to the store where the shopkeeper had grabbed at her genitals through her clothes*], as though she had wanted in that way to provoke the assault. In fact a state of 'oppressive bad conscience' is to be traced back to this experience.

(S.E., p. 354).

What is especially noteworthy about this remark, of course, is that it suggests conflict due to the presence of a sexual impulse at the time of this experience – and the child was only eight – which is in contradiction to his view at that time that sexuality was awakened only in puberty.

COMPROMISE PROCESSES

We now come to see that neuroses are indeed due to a special mix of primary and secondary processes usually referred to as compromises. In neuroses primary processes – compulsion, displacement and isolation – since they arise under conditions of increased load, do not function *in vacuo*. For instance, the concept of compulsion is accompanied by an equally clear statement of the concepts of resistance and repression and a quantitative relationship between them is posited. First the inverse relationship between the substitute and the repressed ideas was stated:

The term 'excessively intense' points to quantitative characteristics. It is plausible to suppose that *repression* has the quantitative meaning of being denuded of Q, and that the sum of the two [of the compulsion and the repression] is equal to the normal. If so, only the distribution has changed. Something has been added to A which has been subtracted from B. The pathological process is one of *displacement*, such as we have come to know in dreams – a primary process therefore.

(S.E., p. 350)

And then the direct relationship between the quantities employed in repression and in resistance:

We can at once recognize in this resistance against B the amount of the *complusion* exercised by A, and we may conclude that the force which in the past repressed B is to be seen here at work once more.

(S.E., p. 351)

The discussion of repression makes clear that the repressed idea is not merely denied access to consciousness, but that it is also prevented from participating in any preconscious secondary processes: first,

We can sum the matter up: A is compulsive, B is repressed (at least from consciousness).

But then:

We now learn that the resistance is directed against thought being in any way concerned with B, even if it [B] has already been made partly conscious. So that instead of excluded from consciousness we may put *excluded from the process of thought*.

(S.E., p. 361)

And:

If we investigate the state of the repressed [idea] B, we discover that that idea is easy to find and bring into consciousness. This is a surprise, for it might well have been supposed that B was really forgotten, that no memory-trace of B remained in ψ. But no, B is a mnemic image like any other; it is

146

not extinguished. But if, as is usual, B is a complex of cathexes, then a *resistance* arises, which is uncommonly large and hard to defeat, against activity of thought with B.

(S.E., p. 351)

It is not so easy to see how Freud came to the idea that the repressive processes operative in the formation of symptoms are produced in response to the kind of primary processes already discussed in the general model; but we may come to this point of view by way of the differentiation between normal and abnormal defence, another illustration of Freud's way of relating a pathological phenomenon to its normal counterpart. We recall from the earlier discussion that 'wishful cathexis to the point of hallucination leads to a complete expenditure of defence' and thus to a 'complete generation of un-pleasure' (S.E., p. 326). Clearly such is not the case in the ordinary hysterical compulsion or convergence, since – at the cost of the symp-tom, it is true – the release of unpleasure is reasonably well controlled.

The *Project* emphasizes that defence in symptom formation is excessive and so considerably different from a normal primary inhibitory process:

. . . that the operative force of this process is *defence* on the part of the ego, which here, however, is performing more than its normal function [p. 352].

(S.E., p. 353)

So that:

. . . there is a defensive process emanating from the *cathected ego* which results in hysterical repression and, along with it, in hysterical compulsion. To that extent the process seems to be differentiated from the ψ primary processes.

(S.E., p. 351)

And yet:

We need an explanation of the fact that in the case of an *ego-process* con-sequences follow which we are accustomed to only [*in the case of*] primary processes.

(S.E., p. 353)

We are faced then with a kind of compromise process in the presence of a cathected ego, which is distinguished from primary processes only by the presence of such an ego. The distinction is one which Freud has raised in connection with a difficult-to-understand footnote in *The Interpretation of Dreams* (1900) and pursued by Gill (1967). One realizes that there appears to be an incongruity in the theory if one focuses on the often heard statement that various primary processes, like

147

displacement, are brought about by defence. Does that mean that the primary process is a result of defence? How does one square this with the idea that the primary process results from the 'release of an inhibition' (*The Interpretation of Dreams*) and the same concept, in the *Project*, that it is the presence of a cathected ego which inhibits the primary process? Is not defence an inhibiting function? The answer lies in making a crucial distinction between defence that arises in the normal operation of the system to prevent unpleasure and that aroused by an overwhelming amount of unpleasure already in existence:

... ψ is in need of an indication that will draw its attention to the re-cathexis of a hostile mnemic image and enable it to obviate, by means of side-cathexis, the consequent release of unpleasure. If ψ is able to put this inhibition into operation soon enough, the release of unpleasure, and at the same time the defence, will be slight; otherwise there will be immense unpleasure and excessive primary defence.

(S.E., p. 325)

A re-examination of the theory of primary defence in the *Project* leads to the realization that the degree of repression and of anxiety release are parallel in primary process defence. For repression, excessive primary process defence, results from a 'complete generation of unpleasure'. The greater the unpleasure released, the greater the primary defence.

Secondary process defence on the other hand results when the ego successfully inhibits the development of anxiety (unpleasure) and in fact the capacity of the ego to inhibit can be progressively called upon depending on the quantity of unpleasure:

... the ego can succeed in inhibiting the passage [of quantity] from a mnemic image to a release of unpleasure by a copious side-cathexis which can be strengthened according to need.

(S.E., p. 324)

There is, as we have seen, clearly spelled out in the *Project* a theory of hierarchies of defence:

... primary *thought-defence* arises, which, in practical thought, takes the release of unpleasure as a signal [p. 326] to leave a particular pathway – that is, to direct the cathexis of attention *elsewhere*.

(S.E., p. 382)

Not only is 'thought-defence' being distinguished from defence against the memory of a painful experience, but primary thought defence is by implication being distinguished from secondary thought defence. Thought defence is directed against smaller quantities of affect than is defence against painful memories, and thought defence has primary and secondary process forms.

An understanding of the difference between primary and secondary process defence sheds light on what are generally regarded as two theories of anxiety. They are summarized by saying that in the first theory repression leads to anxiety, while in the second anxiety leads to repression. As we have just seen, the *Project* clearly enunciates the anxiety leads to repression theory:

. . . the stronger the unpleasure, the stronger will be the primary defence.

(S.E., p. 324)

It seems clear then that the *Project* deals with defence against the generation of unpleasure or, in other words, unpleasure calls forth a defence. But it is primary defence which Freud is talking about here, whereas it is with regard to secondary process defence that we currently say that anxiety (unpleasure) leads to repression (primary defence). These statements make good sense all around, while the 'repression leads to anxiety' theory is harder, though not impossible, to explain in the *Project*'s terms. Recall that primary defence is based on differences in threshold which lead facilitations (the memory-motive structure) away from the key neurons and into motor pathways. As a primary process, such defence is thus based on discharge rather than on inhibition as is secondary process defence. And discharge, even motor discharge, furnishes at best temporary relief from accruing excitation since it often generates affect. Thus the discharge must become repetitive, if it is to be effective as Schur (1966) among others has described. It is in this manner that recourse to excessive primary defence (repression) leads to affect and symptom formation, e.g. repetition compulsion.

Our analysis of these two theories helps explain why Freud remained loath in *Inhibitions, Symptoms and Anxiety* (1926) to give up the anxiety leads to repression theory, referring to the actual neurosis and calling it 'id anxiety', obviously a primary process theory.

We will soon see, in connection with a discussion of 'posthumous' primary processes, why Freud had to postulate *repression antecedent to current unpleasure*, leading to his theory of primal repression.

It should also be pointed out that the slogan 'anxiety leads to repression' (translated into the terminology of the *Project* as 'the generation of unpleasure, a biochemical positive feedback process, leads to a compromise formation in the form of repression'), ably traced by Stewart (1967) in his discussion of the 'toxic theory', does not fare as well as the 'repression leads to anxiety' slogan. But this is in part due to the impact on the toxic theory of the change in emphasis in the description of affect from that of the *Project*, where it was a quantity released by external exigencies activating a memory trace, to the later emphasis where affect became identified exclusively as a drive representation. 'Repression leads to affect' thus became synonymous with 'repression leads to anxiety' which, strictly speaking according to the *Project*, should read 'repression leads to *unpleasure*' not affect.

It is worth noting that repression is by no means the only compromise process which is described:

We shall hear, however, in connection with the analysis of, for instance, obsessional neurosis, that there *repression without* symbol formation occurs, and indeed that there repression and substitution are chronologically separated.

(S.E., p. 352)

Clearly the mechanism of isolation is being referred to. It is also noteworthy that Freud already employed here the term 'substitution', which appears again in detail in the papers on metapsychology and in which the formation of a substitute is defined as the return of the repressed (see Gill, 1963, p. 104).

Thus a careful application of Freud's discussions of dream formation and psychopathology leads to the conclusion that in the adult a primary process can come about in two ways, either through the malfunctioning of the attentional mechanism and reality testing or through a malfunctioning of defences against unpleasure. An adult apparatus functioning according to primary process alone is even according to the *Project* a 'fiction' (see also *The Interpretation of Dreams* and Gill, 1963). A primary process in the presence of a functioning ego, as in symptom formation, means that insofar as there is a primary process, inhibition has been released, but to the extent that there is a compromise formation, inhibition may become enhanced. One may thus see in a successful primary process defence (symptom formation without anxiety) an imposition of inhibition with regard to the thought process (which becomes isolated through the compromise formation) and a release with respect to the production of unexpected affect.

These issues have by no means been thoroughly explored. The root of the problem is that the primary part of the primary-secondary process continuum of defence has been so little emphasized. The paradox focused on so sharply in the *Project* is that a process under the influence of the ego – presumably, then a secondary process – nevertheless shows primary process features. Gill (1963) has dealt with this issue as a failure thoroughly to comprehend the concept of a compromise formation, and more recently Hilgard (1973) has revived interest in the problem by interpreting the results of his experiments on pain reduction in hypnosis in a neodissociation framework. Hilgard's interpretation comes close to that of the *Project* in that dissociation results from a more or less 'vertical' split between hierarchically organized, programmed controls rather than from repression as a 'horizontal' suppression into unconsciousness. Repression is defined in the *Project* as excessive primary defence disrupting the hierarchy of secondary processes and Freud thus proposes a specific mechanism by which such 'vertical' as well as 'horizontal' dissociation can occur. But more on this in the next section.

PREFACE TO CLINICAL THEORY

The remaining major issue of the *Project*, and it is to explicate this that a case is described, is the hypothesis of a posthumous primary process – one which does not take place at the time of the original experience, but does so later in connection with a memory of the experience. The hypothesis was necessitated, as mentioned earlier, by the fact that infantile sexuality had not yet been discovered. The analyses Freud carried out – still under the influence of the seduction hypothesis – led him to sexual 'scenes' (the word used in the *Project*, as in all the early clinical writings, to describe the episode of seduction) antedating puberty. The repression, in Freud's view, took place after puberty, after the establishment of a cathected ego. Once again, then, he had to explain how a primary process could take place in the presence of a well-established ego.

With his customary ingenuity, he demonstrated that matters *had* to be arranged as he saw them, since only thus could they be consistent with his theory. Starting with the premise that there was no release of sexual feeling at the time of the original experience, he pointed out that the experience could not be 'understood' using that term in his special sense of cognition of one's own subjective experience [*Erfahrung*].

As regards judging, there is further to be remarked that its basis is obviously the presence of bodily experiences, sensations and motor images of one's own. So long as these are absent, the variable portion [p. 328] of the perceptual complex remains ununderstood – that is, it can be reproduced but does not point a direction for further paths of thought. Thus, for instance, and this will become important in what follows [in Part II], no sexual experiences produce any effect so long as the subject is ignorant of all sexual feeling – in general, that is, till the beginning of puberty.

(S.E., p. 333)

The absence of sexual feeling at the time of the experience led Freud to the concept of 'delayed affect', since the affect was released when the experience was *remembered,* though not when it was first experienced:

. . . but it is highly noteworthy that it [the sexual release] was not linked to the assault when this was experienced. Here we have the case of a memory arousing an affect which it did not arouse as an experience, because in the meantime the change [brought about] in puberty had made possible a different understanding of what was remembered.

(S.E., p. 356)

Freud left himself an out, however, by suggesting that in some instances the release of sexual affect might be precocious:

We have not been able to reject [the fact] that the disturbance of the normal psychical process had two determinants: (1) that the sexual release was attached to a memory instead of to an experience, (2) that the sexual release took place *prematurely.*

(S.E., p. 357)

And thus the conclusion based on the erroneous clinical idea that sexuality begins with puberty:

The retardation of puberty makes possible posthumous primary processes.

(S.E., p. 359)

But the hypothesis of delayed affect by no means disappeared from Freud's theory with the discovery of infantile sexuality. It is a key concept for example in Freud's explanation of the Wolf-man's responding to the primal scene not at the time of originally experiencing it but with its later activation as a memory (1918).

An important hypothesis dealing with the differences in susceptibility to repression of a memory, in contrast to a percept, is to be found in *The Interpretation of Dreams*:

We find that repression (which, though it served a useful purpose to begin with, leads ultimately to a damaging loss of inhibition and mental control) affects memories so much more easily than perceptions because the former can receive no extra cathexis from the excitation of the psychical sense organs. It is true on the one hand that a thought which has to be warded off cannot become conscious, because it has undergone repression; but on the other hand it sometimes happens that a thought of this kind is only repressed because for other reasons it has been withdrawn from conscious perception. Here are some hints of which we take advantage in our therapeutic procedure in order to undo repressions which have already been effected.

(S.E., vol. 5, p. 617)

In a letter to Oskar Pfister, 10th January 1910, Freud wrote similarly:

All repressions operate on *memories*, not on experiences; the latter are at most repressed only in consequence.

(Jones, 1955, vol. 2, p. 447)

Contemporary theory, of course, emphasizes the repression of both *impulses* and of *memories*. However, as a consequence of the over-weighting of theory on the side of drives there has been an over-emphasis on repression of impulse as opposed to memory.

Freud's explanation of how the delayed affect leads to the posthumous primary process is ingenious and permits him to emphasize the adaptive value of the cathexes of attention:

Attention is [normally] adjusted towards perceptions, which are what ordinarily give occasion for a release of unpleasure. Here, [however, what has appeared] is no perception but a memory, which unexpectedly releases unpleasure, and the ego only discovers this too late. It has permitted a primary process because it did not expect one.

(S.E., p. 358)

And:

Thus it is the ego's business not to permit any release of affect, because this . . . [*raises the possibility of*] a primary process. Its best instrument for this purpose is the mechanism of attention. If a cathexis releasing unpleasure were able to evade this, then the ego would come into action against it too late.

(S.E., p. 358)

An important related hypothesis, but now one without the encumbrance of the theory of delayed affect, appears clearly in the *Project*, and then in the seventh chapter of *The Interpretation of Dreams*. In the former, Freud wrote:

It is therefore only a question of the ego's inhibition not being absent at the *first* release of unpleasure, of the process not occurring as a posthumous primary affective experience . . .

(S.E., p. 359)

Although the term 'posthumous primary process' disappeared from

Freud's theory after the *Project,* in a certain sense the concept did not and has not yet. For it remains in the theory of primal repression, a theory which holds that all secondary repression is based on a store of primally repressed material and that the grounds for the two types of repressions differ. Secondary repression results from anxiety but primal repression, in the revision of the theory of posthumous primary processes, results from the 'belated appearance of the secondary processes'. Freud wrote in *The Interpretation of Dreams*:

The memories on the basis of which the unconscious wish brings about the release of affect were never accessible to the *Pcs.* . . . The unpleasure principle takes control and causes the *Pcs.* to turn away from the transference thoughts. They are left to themselves – 'repressed' – and thus it is that the presence of a store of infantile memories, which have from the first been held back from the *Pcs.*, becomes a *sine qua non* of repression.

(S.E., vol. 5, p. 604)

And:

In consequence of the belated appearance of the secondary processes, the core of our being, consisting of unconscious wishful impulses, remains inaccessible to the understanding and inhibition of the preconscious; the part played by the latter is restricted once and for all to directing along the most expedient paths the wishful impulses that arise from the unconscious. These unconscious wishes exercise a compelling force upon all later mental trends, a force which those trends are obliged to fall in with or which they may perhaps endeavour to divert and direct to higher aims. A further result of the belated appearance of the secondary process is that a wide sphere of mnemic material is inaccessible to preconscious cathexis.

(ibid., pp. 603–4)

It remains a question in our minds whether even this revision is necessary and whether one may not argue that repression in childhood and later too are not both because of conflict and anxiety. Does not this statement in *The Interpretation of Dreams* suffice to cover the facts:

The theory of the psychoneuroses asserts as an indisputable and invariable fact that only sexual wishful impulses from infancy, which have undergone repression (i.e. a transformation of their affect) during the developmental period of childhood, are capable of being revived during *later* developmental periods (whether as a result of the subject's sexual constitution, which is derived from an initial bisexuality, or as a result of unfavourable influences acting upon the course of his sexual life) [*see the emphasis on both constitution and experience*] and are thus able to furnish the motive force for the formation of psychoneurotic symptoms of every kind.

(ibid., pp. 605–6)

It is possible that the distinction between a prepubertal time when there was no release of feeling with a sexual experience and the posthumous release of affect when the memory of this experience is postpubertally awakened may find a reverberation in the theory of altered states of consciousness and the shifts in impulse-defence balances in these altered states. Freud wrote in the *Project*:

It is quite certainly established that two kinds of ψ processes are mixed up together here, that the memory of Scene II (shopkeeper) occurred in quite a different state from the other one.

(S.E., p. 354)

Scene II is the earlier one during which Freud assumed there was no release of sexual feeling, whereas in scene I, the later scene, there was.

The early clinical papers show a clear connection between the concept of special states of consciousness and states of potential heightened affect. Freud's discovery of conflict forced him, for a time, to under-emphasize the importance of states of consciousness – signalized by Breuer's view of the 'hypnoid state' (see articles by Loewald, 1955, and Holzman, 1959) – but what is striking about that part of the *Project* which deals with psychopathology is the number of basic tenets of Freud's clinical theory which are set forth; the manner in which the erroneous concept advanced because infantile sexuality was not yet discovered continues to influence the theory even after its discovery; the strong light therefore shed on obscurities in the theory through the clearer form in which these early hypotheses appear in the *Project*; as well as the material showing that the *Project* is in certain respects, as in the distinction between primary and secondary process defence and a hierarchy of defences, at least as advanced as some segments of current clinical theory.

EPILOGUE:

THE *PROJECT* AND FREUD'S SUBSEQUENT WORK

The 'Project' in History: The impression seems to be widespread among analysts that Freud abandoned the *Project* and the kind of thinking on which it was based and that therefore any serious study of the *Project* can be of only historical interest and unrelated to contemporary psychoanalysis.

We hope to have dispelled this idea by the book itself, but perhaps this section dealing with the evidence that the ideas of the *Project* were never abandoned by Freud will help further to dispel it.

To make our point, we shall first have to propose several clarifications.

The *Project* includes a number of different types of propositions, and it is only with regard to some of them that the question we are discussing arises. There are at least these four types:

1) Psychological propositions like those about repression as a defence;

2) Psychological propositions for which neurological models are provided in the *Project* but not at any later period, like the mechanism by which 'lateral cathexes' change primary into secondary process functioning;

3) Psychological propositions for which neurological models are provided which persist, despite disavowal that a neurological substrate is intended, into Freud's later writings, like the idea that the primary process uses free energy while the secondary process uses bound energy;

4) Neurological and biological assumptions which allegedly are regulatory principles for mental life, like the constancy principle or the idea that the mental apparatus functions like a reflex arc.

Which of these kinds of propositions is Freud alleged to have abandoned? There is, of course, no argument about the psychological propositions. Furthermore, propositions about neurological assumptions like the constancy principle or biological assumptions like those that the driving force of the psychic apparatus is ultimately the somatic instincts remain staples of psychoanalytic thinking.

159

What has been abandoned is clearly part of the neurological model, like lateral cathexes. What is alleged to have been abandoned, but has not, are some of the neurological and biological assumptions which explicitly underlie that part of the *Project* which has become currently accepted metapsychology. The paradigmatic example would be that now the concept of psychic energy is said to have no reference to any physical substratum.

While it is true that the *Project* speaks much more explicitly about the energy concept than do later writings (the leading word in the *Project* is 'excitation'), our task is to show that energy and related concepts continue to have an implicit material (neural or chemical) substratum. It may be asked, what difference does it make. The answer is that the denial of the hidden neurological and biological assumptions conceals the fact that the metapsychology is reductionistic and prevents the disentangling of the psychological and natural science universes of discourse in psychoanalytical propositions. Furthermore, Freud's model has degenerated into a metaphor. That does not mean that it has been shorn of its neurological and biological assumptions. It does mean that the degenerated model is no longer formulated in testable terms, while the loose metaphor is taken as veridical.

DISAVOWALS

Our procedure will be to cite a number of quotations from Freud to show that he continued to regard his metapsychology as both basic and veridical, that is, relating to the actual structure and function of the nervous system.

One of the factors that interferes with the easy demonstration of this point is that Freud frequently explicitly disavowed that his metapsychological concepts were meant to reflect the structure and function of the nervous system – though often, as will be brought out more clearly in the next sections, the disavowal was for the time being only. Some of the disavowals, stated in chronological order, are these:

1) I shall entirely disregard the fact that the mental apparatus with which we are here concerned is also known to us in the form of an anatomical preparation, and I shall carefully avoid the temptation to determine psychical locality in any anatomical fashion. I shall remain on psychological ground. . . .

(*The Interpretation of Dreams*, 1900, S.E., vol. 5, p. 536)

2) It may safely be said that the psycho-analytic study of dreams has given us our first insight into a 'depth-psychology' whose existence had not hitherto been suspected.

And a footnote reads:

Psycho-analysis does not at present postulate any relation between this psychical topography and anatomical stratification or histological layers.'

(*The Claims of Psycho-Analysis to Scientific Interest*, 1913, S.E., vol. 13, p. 171)

3) The quotation most often cited to demonstrate Freud's disavowal is this:

... every attempt to ... discover a localization of mental processes, every endeavour to think of ideas as stored up in nerve-cells and of excitations as travelling along nerve-fibres, has miscarried completely.

(*The Unconscious*, 1915, S.E., vol. 14, p. 174)

4) This is the gap which psycho-analysis seeks to fill. It tries to give psychiatry its missing psychological foundation. It hopes to discover the common ground on the basis of which the convergence of physical and mental disorder will become intelligible. With this aim in view psycho-analysis must keep itself free from any hypothesis that is alien to it, whether of an anatomical, chemical or physiological kind, and must operate entirely with purely psychological auxiliary ideas; and for that very reason, I fear, it will seem strange to you to begin with.

(*Introductory Lectures on Psycho-Analysis*, 1915–16, S.E., vol. 15, p. 21)

5) In lecture 25 on anxiety in the *Introductory Lectures on Psycho-Analysis*, Freud writes:

... you will certainly expect psycho-analysis to approach this subject [anxiety] too in quite a different way from academic medicine. Interest there seems mainly to be centred on tracing the anatomical paths along which the state of anxiety is brought about. We are told that the medulla oblongata is stimulated, and the patient learns that he is suffering from a neurosis of the vagus nerve. The medulla oblongata is a very serious and lovely object. I remember quite clearly how much time and trouble I devoted to its study many years ago. To-day, however, I must remark that I know nothing that could be of less interest to me for the psychological understanding of anxiety than a knowledge of the path of the nerves along which its excitations pass.

(*Introductory Lectures on Psycho-Analysis*, 1916–17, S.E., vol. 16, p. 393)

6) In *An Autobiographical Study*:

The subdivision of the unconscious [*into unconscious and preconscious*] is part of an attempt to picture the apparatus of the mind as being built up by a number of *agencies* or *systems* whose relations to one another are expressed in special terms, without, however, implying any connection with the actual anatomy of the brain.

(1925, S.E., vol. 20, pp. 32–3)

7) In *The Question of Lay Analysis* the interlocutor says: 'What do you mean by the "mental apparatus"? And what, may I ask, is it constructed of?'
    Freud replied:

It will soon be clear what the mental apparatus is; but I must beg you not to ask what material it is constructed of. That is not a subject of psychological interest. Psychology can be as indifferent to it, as for instance, optics can be to the question whether the walls of the telescope are made of metal or cardboard. We shall leave entirely on one side the *material* line of approach but not so the *spatial* one.

(1926, S.E., vol. 20, p. 194)

THE TIME IS NOT YET RIPE

But the quotations to follow make it clear that this disavowal was not one in *principle* but only for the *present*. Freud felt the requisite knowledge to provide the organic substratum for his metapsychological concepts was not yet available but would be at some time in the future. These ideas about a substratum are of two kinds, neurological and biological. Neurologically the stress falls on energy and its differing qualities. Of the two central ideas of the *Project*, quantity and neuron theory, Freud continues to hold to his ideas about quantity and its differing forms, but no longer uses the model of neuron theory. Again the quotations are chronologically arranged:

1) The faithfulness with which the seventh chapter of *The Interpretation of Dreams* follows the *Project* is immediately evident to anyone with even only a cursory acquaintance with the two statements. A typical example which shows how 'associative paths' has become the term which in the *Project* was the neuron network:

Let us add a frank account of how we picture the occurrence of a train of ideas. We believe that, starting from a purposive idea, a given amount of excitation, which we term 'cathectic energy', is displaced along the associative paths selected by that purposive idea.

(1900, S.E., vol. 5, p. 594)

2) The concepts of 'psychical energy' and 'discharge' and the treatment of psychical energy as a quantity have become habitual in my thoughts since I began to arrange the facts of psychopathology philosophically . . .

It is only when I speak of the 'cathexis of psychical paths' that I seem to depart from the analogies commonly used by Lipps. My experiences of displaceability of psychical energy along certain paths of association, and of the almost indestructable persistance of the traces of psychical processes, have in fact suggested to me an attempt at picturing the unknown in some such way. To avoid misunderstanding, I must add that I am making no attempt to proclaim that the cells and nerve fibres, or the systems of neurones which are taking their place today, are these psychical paths, even though it would have to be possible in some manner which cannot yet be indicated to represent such paths by organic elements in the nervous system.

(S.E., vol. 8, p. 147)

3) Freud's natural science assumptions in the *Project* were biological as well as neurological, so some of the quotations like the next one deal with these persisting biological assumptions in Freud's writings.

We have found it necessary to hold aloof from biological considerations during our psycho-analytic work and to refrain from using them for heuristic purposes, so that we may not be misled in our impartial judgement of the psycho-analytic facts before us. But after we have completed our psycho-analytic work we shall have to find a point of contact with biology; and we may rightly feel glad if that contact is already assured at one important point or another.

The contrast between the ego instincts and the sexual instinct [*recall that Freud's term is 'Triebe', 'drive', and therefore may be understood to have less of the connotation of innateness which the mistranslation 'instinct' carries*], to which we have been obliged to trace back the origin of the neuroses, is carried into the sphere of biology in the contrast between the instincts which serve the preservation of the individual and those which serve the survival of the species. . . . It is only this conception which enables us rightly to understand the part played by the sexual instinctual forces in physiology and psychology.

In spite of all our efforts to prevent the biological terminology and considerations from dominating psycho-analytic work, we cannot avoid using them even in our descriptions of the phenomena that we study. . . .

I shall be satisfied if these few remarks have drawn attention to the many respects in which psycho-analysis acts as an intermediary between biology and psychology.

(*The Claims of Psycho-Analysis to Scientific Interest*, 1913, S.E., vol. 13, pp. 181–2)

4) . . . we must recollect that all our provisional ideas in psychology will presumably some day be based on an organic substructure. This makes it probable that it is special substances and chemical processes which perform the operations of sexuality and provide for the extension of individual life into that of the species. . . .

I try in general to keep psychology clear from everything that is different in nature from it, even biological lines of thought. For that very reason I should like at this point expressly to admit that the hypothesis of separate ego instincts and sexual instincts (that is to say, the libido theory) rests scarcely at all upon a psychological basis, but derives its principal support from biology. . . . Since we cannot wait for another science to present us with final conclusions on this theory of the instincts [*drives*], it is far more to the purpose that we should try to see what light may be thrown upon this basic problem of biology by a synthesis of the *psychological* phenomena.

(*On Narcissism*, 1914, S.E., vol. 14, pp. 78–9)

5) The study of the sources of instincts [*drives*] lies outside the scope of psychology. Although instincts are wholly determined by their origin in their somatic source, in mental life we know them only by their aims. An exact knowledge of the sources of an instinct is not invariably necessary for purposes of psychological investigation; sometimes its source may be inferred from its aim.

(*Instincts and their Vicissitudes*, 1915, S.E., vol. 14, p. 123)

6) Freud's distinction between ideas and affects is a neurological one, not one of psychological meaning:

The whole difference arises from the fact that ideas are cathexes – basically of memory-traces – while affects and emotions correspond to processes of discharge, the final manifestations of which are perceived as feelings. In the present state of our knowledge of affects and emotions we cannot express this difference more clearly.

(*The Unconscious*, 1915, S.E., vol. 14, p. 178)

7) The processes of the system *Pcs.* display – no matter whether they are already conscious or only capable of becoming conscious – an inhibition of the tendency of cathected ideas towards discharge. When a process passes from one idea to another, the first idea retains a part of its cathexis and only a small portion undergoes displacement. Displacements and condensations such as happen in the primary process

are excluded or very much restricted. This circumstance caused Breuer to assume the existence of two different states of cathected energy in mental life; one in which the energy is tonically 'bound' and the other in which it is freely mobile and presses towards discharge. In my opinion this distinction represents the deepest insight we have gained up to the present into the nature of nervous energy, and I do not see how we can avoid making it. A metapsychological presentation would most urgently call for further discussion at this point, though perhaps that would be too daring an undertaking as yet.

(ibid., p. 188)

Note also the use of the word metapsychological here which comes very close to equating the employment of the term with neurology.

8) *Beyond the Pleasure Principle* repeats with great fidelity the major natural science assumptions of the *Project*. All that is missing is the neuron model. For the details of the similarity the reader should see Strachey's notes in the Standard Edition, vol. 18. Here is an example which goes so far as to suggest that psychoanalysis can provide an explanation for an anatomical matter which anatomy does not.

In discussing the system '*Pct.-Cs.* [Perception-Consciousness]' in space Freud writes:

It must lie on the borderline between outside and inside; it must be turned towards the external world and must envelop the other psychical systems. It will be seen that there is nothing daringly new in these assumptions; we have merely adopted the views on localization held by cerebral anatomy, which locates the 'seat' of consciousness in the cerebral cortex – the outermost, enveloping layer of the central organ. Cerebral anatomy has no need to consider why, speaking anatomically, consciousness should be lodged on the surface of the brain instead of being safely housed somewhere in its inmost interior. Perhaps *we* shall be more successful in accounting for this situation in the case of our system *Pcpt.-Cs.* [Perception-Consciousness].

(*Beyond the Pleasure Principle*, 1920, S.E., vol. 18, p. 24)

9) The indefiniteness of all our discussions on what we describe as metapsychology is of course due to the fact that we know nothing of the nature of the excitatory process that takes place in the elements of the psychical systems, and that we do not feel justified in framing any hypothesis on the subject. We are consequently operating all the time with a large unknown factor, which we are obliged to carry over into every new formula. It may be reasonably supposed that this excitatory process can be carried out with energies that vary *quantitatively*; it may also seem probable that it has more than one *quality* (in the nature of amplitude, for instance). As a new factor we have taken into consideration Breuer's hypothesis that the charges of energy occur in two forms . . .; so that we have to distinguish between two kinds of cathexis of the psychical systems or their elements – of freely flowing cathexis that press on towards discharge and a quiescent cathexis. We may perhaps suspect that the binding of the energy that streams into the mental apparatus consists in its change from a free flowing into a quiescent state.

(ibid., pp. 30–31)

In this monograph we emphasize the distinction between current in flow and local graded potentials as a major feature of the *Project*. Here we have the formulation of 1895 repeated in 1920.

10) The importance Freud gave to this idea whose origin he attributed to Breuer is also stated in an encyclopedia article written in 1920:

In a theoretical section of the *Studies* Breuer brought forward some speculative ideas about the processes of excitation of the mind. These ideas determined the direction of future lines of thought and even to-day have not received sufficient appreciation.

(*Two Encyclopaedia Articles*, 1923, S.E., vol. 18, p. 236)

11) The last quotation of this series is from the *New Introductory Lectures* of 1933:

. . . I must admit that I have tried to translate into the language of our normal thinking what must in fact be a process that is neither conscious or preconscious, taking place between quotas of energy in some unimaginable substratum.

What Freud was talking about was how

the ego anticipates the satisfaction of the questionable instinctual impulse and permits it to bring about the reproduction of the unpleasurable feelings at the beginning of the feared situation of danger. With this the automatism of the pleasure-unpleasure principle is brought into operation and now carries out the repression of the dangerous instinctual impulse.

(*New Introductory Lectures on Psycho-Analysis*, 1933, S.E., vol. 22, pp. 89–90)

THE NEUROCHEMISTRY OF NEUROSES AND PSYCHOSES

Yet another line of thought which can be followed in Freud's writings to demonstrate his persisting neurological and biological assumptions are his statements of a possible future organic therapy for the neuroses. These too will be given in chronological order. It will be seen that he sometimes anticipates that such therapies will one day be available but on other occasions is doubtful. The issue of whether such a therapy would be possible *in principle* he does not tackle.

1) This first quotation compares the neuroses to organic intoxications:

We have been led on imperceptibly from the question of the causation of the psychoneuroses to the problem of their essential nature. If we are prepared to take into account what has been learnt from psycho-analysis, we can only say that the essence of these illnesses lies in disturbances of the sexual processes, the processes which determine in the organism the formation and utilization of sexual libido. It is scarcely possible to avoid picturing these processes as being in the last resort of a chemical nature; so that in what I termed the 'actual' neuroses we may recognize the *somatic* effects of disturbances of the sexual metabolism, and in the psychoneuroses the *psychical* effects of those disturbances as well. The similarity of the neuroses to the phenomena of intoxication and abstinence after the use of certain alkaloids, as well as to Graves' disease and Addison's disease, is forced upon our notice clinically. And just as these last two illnesses should no longer be described as 'nervous diseases', so also the 'neuroses' proper, in spite of their name, may soon have to be excluded from that category as well.

(*Sexuality in the Neuroses*, 1906, S.E., vol. 7, pp. 278–9)

2) The same view is repeated in 1917:

In view of these analogies, we cannot, I think, avoid regarding neuroses as results of disturbances in the sexual metabolism, whether because more of these sexual toxins is produced than the subject can deal with, or whether because internal and even psychical conditions restrict the proper employment of these substances. . . . And for us this would be an occasion for recalling the erotogenic zones and our assertion that sexual excitation can be generated in the most various organs. . . . But for the rest a phrase 'sexual metabolism' or 'chemistry of sexuality' is a term without content: we know nothing about it and cannot even decide whether we are to assume two sexual substances, which would then be named 'male' and 'female', or whether we could be satisfied with *one* sexual toxin which we should have to recognize as a vehicle of all the stimulant effects of libido. The theoretical structure of psycho-analysis that we have created is in truth a superstructure, which will one day have to be set upon its organic foundation. But we are still ignorant of this. . . . The problems of the 'actual' neuroses, whose symptoms are probably generated by direct toxic damage, offer psycho-analysis no points of attack. It can do little towards throwing light on them and must leave the task to biologico-medical research.

(*Introductory Lectures on Psycho-Analysis*, 1916–17, S.E., vol. 16, pp. 388–9)

3) In so far as analytic therapy does not make it its first task to remove the symptoms, it is behaving like a causal therapy. In another respect, you may say, it is not. For we long ago traced the causal chain back through the repressions to the instinctual dispositions, their relative intensities in the constitution and the deviations in the course of their development. Supposing, now, that it was possible, by some chemical means, perhaps, to interfere in this mechanism, to increase or diminish the quantity of libido present at a given time or to strengthen one instinct at the cost of another – this then would be a causal therapy in the true sense of the word, for which our analysis would have carried out the indispensable preliminary work of reconnaissance. At present, as you know, there is no question of any such method of influencing libidinal processes; with our psychical therapy we attack at a different point in the combination – not exactly at what we know are the roots of the phenomena, but nevertheless far enough away from the symptoms, at a point which has been made accessible to us by some very remarkable circumstances.

(ibid., vol. 16, p. 436)

4) It is to be feared that our need to find a single, tangible 'ultimate cause' of neurotic illness will remain unsatisfied. The ideal solution, which medical men no doubt still yearn for, would be to discover some bacillus which could be isolated and bred in pure culture and which, when injected into anyone, would invariably produce the same illness; or to put it rather less extravagantly, to demonstrate the existence of

certain chemical substances the administration of which would bring about or cure particular neuroses. But the probability of a solution of this kind seems slight.

(*Inhibitions, Symptoms and Anxiety*, 1926, S.E., vol. 20, pp. 152–3)

5) In view of the intimate connection between the things that we distinguish as physical and mental, we may look forward to the day when paths of knowledge and, let us hope, of influence will be opened up, leading from organic biology and chemistry to the field of neurotic phenomena. That day still seems a distant one, and for the present these illnesses are inaccessible to us from the direction of medicine.

(*The Question of Lay Analysis*, 1926, S.E., vol. 20, p. 231)

All too often one seems to see that it is only the treatment's lack of the necessary motive force that prevents one from bringing the change about. One particular dependent relation, one special instinctual component, is too powerful in comparison with the opposing forces that we are able to mobilize. This is quite generally true with the psychoses. We understand them well enough to know the point at which the levers should be applied, but they would not be able to move their weight. It is here, indeed, that hope for the future lies: the possibility that our knowledge of the operation of the hormones (you know what they are) may give us the means of successfully combating the quantitative factors of the illnesses; but we are far from that today.

(ibid.)

6) Biological factors subsequently deflect those libidinal forces [in the girl's case] from their original aims and conduct even active and in every sense masculine trends into feminine channels. Since we cannot dismiss the notion that sexual excitation is derived from the operation of certain chemical substances, it seems plausible at first to expect that biochemistry will one day disclose a substance to us whose presence produces the male sexual excitation and another substance which produces a female one. But this hope seems no less naïve than the other one – happily obsolete today – that it may be possible under the microscope to isolate the different exciting factors of hysteria, obsessional neurosis, melancholia, and so on.

(*Female Sexuality*, 1931, S.E., vol. 21, p. 240)

And two pages later:

... the only role left to the former [*original impulses*] is merely to indicate certain paths, while the [psychical] intensities which flow along those paths are supplied by later regressions and reaction-formations.

(ibid., pp. 242–3)

Strachey adds a footnote with regard to the word 'intensity' that

Freud does not often use the word, as here, without any qualifying epithet: '*Psychische Intensität*' occurs very often in *The Interpretation of Dreams*. . . . It seems, on the whole, likely that Freud is in fact using the word as an equivalent to the term 'quantity' which he preferred in the earlier 'Project' of 1895. . . . He seemed actually to use the two terms as synonyms towards the beginning of Section (2) of his second paper on anxiety neurosis (1895), *Standard Ed.*, **3**. The term 'quantity' is equated in the metapsychological paper on 'Repression' (1915) with 'instinctual energy'.

IN CONCLUSION

It is our opinion, therefore, that Freud felt

1) that psychoanalysis had to become established as a purely psychological discipline using behavioural observations and the analysis of verbal reports as its techniques;

2) that ultimately this psychoanalytic science could be rejoined to its biochemical and neurological origins, but that a) the time was not right and b) this rejoining would *not* be a simplistic 'taking over' or 'reductive explanation' of psychoanalytic knowledge in biochemical or neurophysiological terms.

3) Furthermore, we feel that Freud often recognized that his metapsychological propositions were based on neurological and biological assumptions but sometimes failed to recognize this and even explicitly disavowed that it was so.

The two authors of this monograph agree that it would have been better for Freud to have published the *Project* and then set it aside rather than let it fester unseen to degenerate into untestable metaphor that repeatedly and unpredictably bursts to the surface in later theorizing.

However, we are still in some disagreement as to whether the time is now ripe for rapprochement between psychoanalysis, experimental psychology, neurophysiology and neurochemistry. More accurately, we disagree as to whether the time will *ever* be right or whether these disciplines – as different levels of inquiry and explanation, one in the universe of human meaning and the other in the universe of natural science – must inevitably go their separate ways.

Reductive explanation of psychoanalytic knowledge is not what either of us espouses. Pribram, however, feels there is a place in the scientific scheme for investigators and practitioners working at the interface between disciplines. Further, he feels that often, though not always, the most significant advances in understanding and in practice arise at such interfaces. Pribram proposes two examples: the meaning of a phrase of music is certainly largely independent of the characteristics of the medium in which that music is realized; a high-level programmer can function reasonably well without knowing whether his program is going to be realized with an IBM or a CDC computer. But *somebody* has to know – a conductor, a taping expert, an assembler of machine language, etc. – else the music and program remain unrealized. Gill feels, on the other hand, that a knowledge of the medium in which the music or program is realized tells us nothing about the music *as music* or the program *as program*.

Pribram feels it is important that this volume addresses and finds audience in these 'somebodies' working at the brain-behaviour-experience interfaces.

Specifically, he urges psychologists in the physiological and in the cognitive areas to review the *Project* for currently relevant, comprehensive and detailed theories of thinking and consciousness. Gill also feels that they ought to read it, and that psychoanalysts will profit by sympathetic study of Freud's *Project* because it is, in important respects, considerably more explicit than Chapter 7 of *The Interpretation of Dreams* – their current source for meta-psychological understanding. Where we differ is that Gill feels that psycho-analysis must go its own way and that means purging it of its natural science metapsychology, while Pribram welcomes psychoanalysis back into the natural sciences. Pribram doubts that the differing views of the two authors are really, in the long run, incompatible, while Gill finds them irreconcilable.

BIBLIOGRAPHY

All quotations from Freud's works are, with the exception of the extracts from his letters, taken from Volume 1 (unless otherwise noted) of the *Standard Edition of the Complete Psychological Works of Sigmund Freud*, edited and translated by James Strachey, Hogarth Press, twenty-four volumes. The individual works are listed in the bibliography below. In the quotations Strachey's editorial additions are enclosed in square brackets and set in roman type; additions by the present authors are enclosed in square brackets and set in italic type.

The extracts from Freud's letters to Wilhelm Fliess are taken from the Standard Edition or from *The Origins of Psycho-Analysis. Letters to Wilhelm Fliess, Drafts and Notes 1887–1904*, Imago, Basic Books, 1954.

Adams, R. 1969, The anatomy of memory mechanisms in the human brain, *The Pathology of Memory*, G. A. Talland and N. C. Waugh (eds.). New York: Academic Press, pp. 91–106.

Adey, W. R., Kado, R. T., Didio, J. and Schindler, W. J. 1963, Impedance changes in cerebral tissue accompanying learned discriminative performance in the cat, *Exp. Neurol.*, 7:259–81.

Albe-Fessard, D. and Kruger, L. 1962, Duality of unit discharges from cat centrum medianum in response to natural and electrical stimulation, *J. Neurophysiol.*, 25: 3–20.

Amacher, P. 1965, Freud's neurological education and its influence on psychoanalytic theory, *Psychological Issues*, No. 4: Mono. 16.

Ashby, W. R. 1960 (2nd edn), *Design for a Brain: The Origin of Adaptive Behavior*. New York: John Wiley & Sons.

Ashby, W. R. 1963, *An Introduction to Cybernetics*. New York: John Wiley & Sons.

Bartlett, F. 1958, *Thinking*. New York: Basic Books, Inc.

Bechterev, W. von 1899, *Die Leitungsbahnen im gehirn und Ruckenmark*. Leipsig: Arthur Georgi.

Beranrd, C. 1858, *Leçons sur la physiologie et la pathologie du système nerveux*, Lecture, 16, vol. II. Paris: Baillière.

Bernfeld, S. 1949, Freud's scientific beginnings, *American Imago*, 6:163–96.

Beurle, R. L. 1956, Properties of a mass of cells capable of regenerating pulses, *Philos. Trans. Royal Soc.* London, 240:55–94.

Bishop, G. 1956, Natural history of the nerve impulse, *Physiol. Rev.*, 36: 376–99.

Blakemore, C. 1974, Developmental factors in the formation of feature extracting neurons, *The Neurosciences Third Study Program*, F. O. Schmitt and F. G. Worden (eds.). Cambridge: MIT Press, pp. 105–13.

Blakemore, C. and Cooper, G. 1970, Development of the brain depends on the visual environment, *Nature*, 228: 477–8.

Brillouin, L. 1962 (2nd edn), *Science and Information Theory*. New York: Academic Press, Inc.

Broadbent, D. E. 1973, *In Defence of Empirical Psychology*. London: Methuen & Co., Ltd.

Brobeck, J. R. 1963, Review and Synthesis, *Brain and Behavior*, vol. II, M. A. B. Brazier (ed.). Washington: American Institute of Biological Sciences, pp. 389–409.

Broca, P. 1878, Anatomie comparée des circonvolutions cérébrales. Le grand lobe limbique et la scissure limbique dans la série des mammifères, *Rev. Anthrop.*, ser. 2, 1:385–498.

Bruner, Jerome S. 1957, On perceptual readiness, *Psychol. Rev.*, 64: 123–52.

Bullock, T. H. 1958, Parameters of integrative action of the nervous system at the neuronal level, *Exp. Cell Research*, 5:323–37.

Cannon, W. B. 1927, The James-Lange theory of emotions: a critical examination and an alternative theory, *Amer. J. Psychol*, 39:106–24.

Cannon, W. B. 1929, *Bodily Changes in Pain, Horror, Fear and Rage. An Account of Recent Researches into the Function of Emotional Excitement*. New York: D. Appleton and Co.

Caton, R. 1875, The electric current of the brain, *Brit. Med. J.*, 2: 278–96.

Colby, K. M. 1955, *Energy and Structure in Psychoanalysis*. New York: Ronald Press.

duBois-Reymond, E. 1849, *Untersuchungen über tierische Elektricität*, vol. II. Berlin: G. Reimer.

Ebbinghaus, H. 1885, *Über das Gedachtnis: Untersuchungen zur experimentellen Psychologie*. Leipzig.

Eccles, J. C. 1964, *The Physiology of Synapses*. Berlin: Springer.

Eccles, J. C. 1967, Postsynaptic inhibition in the central nervous system, *The Neurosciences*, G. C. Quarton, T. Melnechuk and F. O. Schmitt (eds.). New York: Rockefeller University Press, pp. 408–27.

Eccles, J. C. 1970, *Facing Reality*. New York: Springer-Verlag.

Eccles, J. C., Ito, M. and Szentagothai, J. 1967, *The Cerebellum as a Neuronal Machine*. New York: Springer-Verlag.

Exner, S. 1894, *Entwurf zu einer physiologischen Erklärung der psychischen Erscheinungen*. Vienna: Deuticke.

Fancher, R. 1971, The neurological origin of Freud's theory, *J. Hist. Beh. Sci.*, 7:59–74.

Foerster, H. von 1965, Memory without record, *The Anatomy of Memory*, D. P. Kimble (ed.). Palo Alto: Science and Behavior Books, Inc., pp. 388–433.

Freud, S. 1891, *On Aphasia*. New York: International Universities Press (1953).

Freud, S. 1894, *The Neuro-Psychoses of Defence*. Standard Edition, vol. 3 (1962), pp. 45–61.

Freud, S. 1895, *On the Grounds for Detaching a Particular Syndrome from Neurasthenia Under the Description 'Anxiety Neurosis'*. Standard Edition, vol. 3 (1962), pp. 90–117.

Freud, S. 1895, *Project for a Scientific Psychology*. Standard Edition, vol. 1 (1966), pp. 281–397.

Freud, S. with Breuer, J. 1895, *Studies on Hysteria*. Standard Edition, vol. 2 (1955).

Freud, S. 1900, *The Interpretation of Dreams*. Standard Edition, vols. 4–5 (1953).

Freud, S. 1905, *Three Essays on the Theory of Sexuality*. Standard Edition, vol. 7 (1953), pp. 126–243.

Freud, S. 1906, *My Views on the Part Played by Sexuality in the Aetiology of the Neuroses*. Standard Edition, vol. 7 (1953), pp. 269–79.

Freud, S. 1911, *Formulations on the Two Principles of Mental Functioning*. Standard Edition, vol. 12 (1958), pp. 218–26.

Freud, S. 1913, *The Claims of Psycho-Analysis to Scientific Interest*. Standard Edition, vol. 13 (1955), pp. 161–90.

Freud, S. 1914, *On Narcissism: An Introduction*. Standard Edition, vol. 14 (1957), pp. 67–102.

Freud, S. 1915, *Instincts and their Vicissitudes*. Standard Edition, vol. 14 (1957), pp. 117–40.

Freud, S. 1915, *Repression*. Standard Edition, vol. 14 (1957), pp. 143–58.

Freud, S. 1915, *The Unconscious*. Standard Edition, vol. 14 (1957), pp. 159–215.

Freud, S. 1915–16, *Introductory Lectures on Psycho-Analysis*, Parts I and II. Standard Edition, vol. 15 (1963).

Freud, S. 1916–17, *Introductory Lectures on Psycho-Analysis*, Part III. Standard Edition, vol. 16 (1963).

Freud, S. 1918, *From the History of an Infantile Neurosis*. Standard Edition, vol. 17 (1955), pp. 7–122.

Freud, S. 1920, *Beyond the Pleasure Principle*. Standard Edition, vol. 18 (1955), pp. 3–64.

Freud, S. 1923, *Two Encyclopaedia Articles*. Standard Edition, vol. 18 (1955), pp. 235–59.

Freud, S. 1925, *An Autobiographical Study*. Standard Edition, vol. 20 (1959), pp. 1–74.

Freud, S. 1926, *Inhibitions, Symptoms and Anxiety*. Standard Edition, vol. 20 (1959), pp. 87–172.

Freud, S. 1926, *The Question of Lay Analysis*. Standard Edition, vol. 20 (1959), pp. 177–258.

Freud, S. 1931, *Female Sexuality*. Standard Edition, vol. 21 (1961), pp. 223–43.

Freud, S. 1933, *New Introductory Lectures on Psycho-Analysis*. Standard Edition, vol. 22 (1964), pp. 3–182.

Freud, S. 1940, *An Outline of Psycho-Analysis*. Standard Edition, vol. 23 (1964), pp. 141–207.

Freud. S. 1954, *The Origins of Psycho-Analysis. Letters to Wilhelm Fliess, Drafts and Notes 1887–1904*. London: Imago; New York: Basic Books.

Gerard, R. W. 1949, Physiology and psychiatry, *Am. J. Psychiat.*, 106: 161–73.

Gerard, R. W. 1950, Some aspects of neural growth, regeneration, and function, *Genetic Neurology*, P. Weiss (ed.). Chicago: University of Chicago Press, pp. 199–207.

Gerard, R. W. 1960, Neurophysiology: An integration (molecules, neurons and behavior), *Handbook of Physiology*, vol. III, J. Field (ed.). Washington: American Physiological Society, pp. 1919–65.

Gibson, J. J. 1966, *The Senses Considered as Perceptual Systems*. Boston: Houghton Mifflin Co.

Gill, M. 1963, *Topography and systems in psychoanalytic theory, Psychological Issues*, No. 10. New York: International Universities Press.

Gill, M. 1967, The primary process, *Motives and Thought*, R. Holt (ed.), *Psychological Issues*, Nos. 18/19. New York: International Universities Press, pp. 259–98.

Gill, M. 1976, Metapsychology is not psychology, *Psychology vs Metapsychology*, M. Gill and P. Halzman (eds.), *Psychological Issues*, No. 36. New York: International Universities Press, in press.

Gloor, P. 1955, Electrophysiological studies on connections of the amygdaloid nucleus in the cat, II, the electrophysiological properties of the amygdaloid projection system, *Electroenceph. Clin. Neurophysiol.*, 7:243–64.

Glover, E. 1947, *Basic Mental Concepts*. London: Imago Publishing Co.

Grey-Walter, W. 1973, Human frontal lobe function in sensory-motor association. *Psychophysiology of the Frontal Lobes*, K. H. Pribram and A. R. Luria (eds.). New York: Academic Press, pp. 109–22.

Hartmann, H. 1958, *Ego Psychology and the Problem of Adaptation*. New York: International Universities Press.

Hebb, D. O. 1949 (1st edn.), *The Organization of Behavior, A Neuropsychological Theory*. New York: John Wiley & Sons, 1961.

Helmholtz, H. von 1867, *Handbuch der physiologischen Optik*. Leipzig: Voss.

Hilgard, E. R. 1973, A neodissociation interpretation of pain reduction in hypnosis, *Psychol. Rev.*, 80:396–411.

Hirsch, H. and Spinelli, D. N. 1970, Distribution of receptive field orientation: modification contingent on conditions of visual experience, *Science*, 168: 869–71.

Holst, E. von 1954, Relations between the central nervous system and the peripheral organs, *Brit. J. Anim. Behav.*, 2: 89–94.

Holst, E. von and Mittelstaedt, H. 1950, Das Reafferenzprinzip., *Naturwissenschaften*, 37: 464–76.

Holt, R. R. (ed.) 1967, *Motives and Thought: Psychoanalytic Essays in Honor of David Rapaport, Psychological Issues*, Nos. 18/19. New York: International Universities Press.

Holzman. P. 1959, A note on Breuer's hypnoidal theory of neurosis, *Bull. Menninger Clinic*, 23: 144–7.

Jacobsen, M. 1970, Development, specification, and diversification of neural connections, *The Neurosciences II*, F.O. Schmitt (ed.). New York: Rockefeller University Press, pp. 116–29.

Jahoda, M. 1972, Social psychology and psychoanalysis: A mutual challenge, *Bull. Brit. Psychol. Soc.*, 25(89): 269–74.

Jones, E. 1953, 1955, 1957, *The Life and Work of Sigmund Freud*, 3 vols. London: Hogarth Press; New York: Basic Books.

Kahneman, D. 1973, *Attention and Effort*. Englewood Cliffs, New Jersey: Prentice-Hall.

Kanzer, M. 1973, Two prevalent misconceptions about Freud's Project (1895), *Annual of Psychoanalysis*, vol. I. New York: Quadrangle/The New York Times Book Co., pp. 88–103.

Karplus, J. P. and Kreidl, A. 1909, Gehirn und Sympathicus, I, Zwischenhirnbasis und halssympathicus, *Arch. ges. Physiol. Pflügers*, 129: 138–44 (246).

Klein, G. 1967, Peremptory Ideation, *Motives and Thought*, R. Holt (ed.), *Psychological Issues*, Nos. 18/19. New York: International Universities Press, pp. 78–128.

Klein, G. 1970, *Perception, Motives, and Personality*. New York: Alfred Knapp.

Kruger, L. and Michel, F. 1962, A single neuron analysis of buccal cavity representation in the sensory trigeminal complex of the cat, *Arch. Oral Biol.*, 7: 491–503.

Kruger, L., Siminoff, R. and Witkovsky, P. 1961, Single neuron analysis of dorsal column nuclei and spinal nucleus of trigeminal in cat, *J. Neurophysiol.*, 24: 333–49.

Lashley, K. S. 1942, The problem of cerebral organization in vision, *Biological Symposia*, vol. III: *Visual Mechanisms*. Lancaster: Jaques Cattell Press, pp. 301–22.

Lewin, B. 1955, Dream psychology and the analytic situation, *Psychoanal. Quart.*, 24:169–99.

Liebeskind, J. C., Mayer, D. J. and Akil, H. 1974, Central mechanisms of pain inhibition: Studies of analgesia from focal brain stimulation, *Advances in Neurology*, vol. IV: *Pain*, J. J. Bonica (ed.). New York: Raven Press.

M

Lindsley, D. B. 1961, The reticular activating system and perceptual integration, *Electrical Stimulation of the Brain*, D. E. Sheer (ed.). Austin: University of Texas Press, pp. 331–49.

Loewald, H. 1955, Hypnoid state, repression, abreaction and recollection, *J. Amer. Psycholanaly. Assoc.*, 3: 201–10.

Lorenz, K. 1937, Über die Bildung des Instinkbegriffes, *Naturwissenschaften*, 25:289–300, 307–18, 324–31.

Lorenz, K. 1950, The comparative method in studying innate behavior patterns, *Symp. Soc. Exp. Biol.*, 4: 221–68.

McDougall, W. 1923, *Outline of Psychology*. San Francisco: Charles Scribner's Sons.

McFarland, D. J. 1971, *Feedback Mechanisms in Animal Behavior*. London: Academic Press.

MacKay, D. M. 1969, *Information, Mechanism and Meaning*. Cambridge: MIT Press.

Magoun, H. W. 1958, *The Waking Brain*. Springfield, Ill.: Charles C. Thomas.

Marx, Otto M. 1970, Freud and Aphasia: An Historical Analysis, *Am. J. Psychiat.*, December.

Mayr, E. 1961, Cause and effect in biology, *Science*, 134: 1501.

Mayr, E. 1971, *Populations, Species, and Evolution*. Cambridge: The Belknap Press of Harvard University Press.

Melzack, R. and Wall, P. D. 1965, Pain mechanisms: A new theory, *Science*, 150: 971–9.

Merlan, P. 1945, Brentano and Freud, *Journal of the History of Ideas*, 6: 375.

Merlan, P. 1949, Brentano and Freud, A sequel, *Journal of the History of Ideas*, 10:451.

Meynert, R. 1890, *Klinische Vorlesungen Über Psychiatrie*. Vienna: Braunmuller.

Miller, G. A. 1953, What is information measurement? *Amer. Psychol.*, 8: 3–11.

Miller, G. A., Galanter, E. H. and Pribram, K. H. 1960, *Plans and the Structure of Behavior*. New York: Henry Holt and Co.

Milner, B. and Penfield, W. 1955, The effect of hippocampal lesions on recent memory, *Trans. Am. Neurol. Assoc.*, 80: 42–8.

Milner, P. M. 1957, The cell assembly: Mark II, *Psychol. Rev.*, 64: 242–52.

Mittelstaedt, H. 1968, Discussion, *Experience and Capacity*, D. P. Kimble (ed.). New York: The New York Academy of Sciences, Interdisciplinary Communications Program, pp. 46–9.

Neisser, U. 1967, *Cognitive Psychology*. New York: Appleton-Century-Crofts.

Perkel, D. H. and Bullock, T. H. 1968, Neural coding, *Neurosciences Res. Prog. Bull*, 6: 221–348.

Peterfreund, E. and Schwartz, J. T. 1971, *Information, systems, and psychoanalysis: An evolutionary biological approach to psychoanalytic theory*, *Psychological Issues*, No. 7: Mono. 25/26.

Pflüger, E. F. W. 1859, *Untersuchungen uber die Physiologie des Elektrotonus.* Berlin: A. Hirschwald.

Pittendrigh, C. S. 1958, Adaptation, natural selection and behavior, *Behavior and Evolution,* A. Roe and G. G. Simpson (eds.). New Haven: Yale University Press, pp. 390–416.

Pribram, K. H. 1959, On the neurology of thinking, *Behav. Sci.,* 4: 265–87.

Pribram, K. H. 1960, A review of theory in physiological psychology, *Annual Review of Psychology.* Palo Alto: Annual Reviews, Inc., vol. 11, pp. 1–40.

Pribram, K. H. 1962, The neuropsychology of Sigmund Freud, *Experimental Foundations of Clinical Psychology,* A. J. Bachrach (ed.). New York: Basic Books, pp. 442–68.

Pribram, K. H. 1965, Freud's *Project*: An open, biologically based model for psychoanalysis, *Psychoanalysis and Current Biological Thought,* N. S. Greenfield and W. C. Lewis (eds.). Madison: University of Wisconsin Press, pp. 81–92.

Pribram, K. H. 1967(a), Memory and the organization of attention, *Brain Function,* vol. IV, D. B. Lindsley and A. A. Lumsdaine (eds.). Berkeley and Los Angeles: University of California Press, pp. 79–122.

Pribram, K. H. 1967(b), The new neurology and the biology of emotion: a structural approach, *Amer. Psychol.,* 22: 830–38.

Pribram, K. H. 1969, The amnestic syndromes: disturbance in coding? *Pathology of Memory,* G. A. Talland and H. C. Waugh (eds.). New York: Academic Press, pp. 127–57.

Pribram, K. H. 1971, *Languages of the Brain: Experimental Paradoxes and Principles in Neuropsychology,* Englewood Cliffs, New Jersey: Prentice-Hall Inc.

Pribram, K. H., Ahumada, A., Hartog, J. and Roos, L. 1964, A progress report on the neurological process disturbed by frontal lesions in primates, *The Frontal Granular Cortex and Behavior,* I. M. Warren and K. Akert (eds.). New York: McGraw-Hill Book Company, Inc., pp. 28–55.

Pribram, K. H. and Broadbent, D. E. (eds.) 1970, *Biology of Memory.* New York: Academic Press.

Pribram, K. H. and Luria, A. R. (eds.) 1973, *Psychophysiology of the Frontal Lobes.* New York: Academic Press.

Pribram, K. H. and McGuinness, D. 1975, Arousal, activation and effort in the control of attention, *Psychol. Rev.* 82(2): 116–49.

Purpura, D. P. 1962, *Brain and Behavior,* vol. II. M. A. B. Brazier (ed.). Washington: American Institute of Biological Sciences.

Rapaport, D. 1950(a), *Emotion and Memory,* 2nd unaltered edition. New York: International Universities Press.

Rapaport, D. 1950(b), Review of *Cybernetics* by Norbert Wiener, *Psychoanalytic Quarterly,* 19: 598–603.

Rapaport, D. (ed. and trans.) 1951, *Organization and Pathology of Thought*. New York: Columbia University Press.

Rapaport, D. 1953, On the psychoanalytic theory of affects, *Internat. J. Psychoanal.* 34: 177–98.

Rapaport. D. 1960, *The structure of psychoanalytic theory, Psychological Issues*, No. 6. New York: International Universities Press.

Rapaport, D. 1961, On the psychoanalytic theory of motivation, *Nebraska Symposium on Motivation*, M. Jones (ed.). University of Nebraska Press, pp. 173–247.

Rapaport, D. and Gill, M. 1959, The points of view and assumptions of metapsychology, *Internat. J. Psychoanal.*, 40: 153–62.

Reitman, W. R. 1965, *Cognition and Thought*. New York: John Wiley & Sons.

Riesen, A. H. 1970, Neuropsychological consequences of altered sensory inputs, *Biology of Memory*, K. H. Pribham and D. E. Broadbent (eds.). New York: Academic Press, pp. 87–99.

Rubenstein, B. 1967, Explanation and mere description, *Motives and Thought*, R. Holt (ed.), *Psychological Issues*, Nos. 18/19. New York: International Universities Press.

Schäfer, E. A. 1900, *Textbook of Physiology*, vol. 2. Edinburgh: Young J. Pentland.

Schafer, R. 1973(a), Action: Its place in psychoanalytic interpretation and theory, *Annual of Psychoanalysis*, vol. I. New York: Quadrangle /The New York Times Book Co., pp. 159–96.

Schafer, R. 1973(b), The idea of resistance, *Internat. J. Psychoanal.*, 54: 259-85.

Schur, M. 1966, *The Id and the Regulatory Principles of Mental Functioning*. New York: International Universities Press.

Sechenov, I. M. 1863, *Reflexes of the Brain*. Cambridge: MIT Press (1965).

Selfridge, O. G. (1959). Pandemonium: a paradigm for learning, *The Mechanization of the Thought Process*. London: H.M.S.O.

Shannon, C. E. and Weaver, W. 1949, *The Mathematical Theory of Communication*. Urbana: University of Illinois Press.

Sherrington, C. 1947, *The Integrative Action of the Nervous System*. New Haven: Yale University Press.

Skinner, J. E. and Lindsley, D. B. 1973, The non-specific mediothalamic-frontocortical system: its influence on electrocortical activity and behavior, *Psychophysiology of the Frontal Lobes*, K. H. Pribram and A. R. Luria (eds.). New York: Academic Press, pp. 185–234.

Sokolov, E. N. 1960, Neuronal models and the orienting reflex, *The Central Nervous System and Behavior*, M. A. B. Brazier (ed.). New York: Josiah Macy Jr Foundation, pp. 187–276.

Sperry, R. W. 1969, A modified concept of consciousness, *Psychol Rev.*, 76: 532–636.

Stent, G. S. 1973, A physiological mechanism for Hebb's postulate of learning, *Proc. Nat. Acad. Sci.*, 70(4): 997–1001.

Stewart, W. 1967, *Psychoanalysis: The First Ten Years, 1888–1898*. New York: Macmillan Co.

Strachey, J. 1955–1966, *The Standard Edition of the Complete Psychological Works of Sigmund Freud*, 24 vols. London: The Hogarth Press Ltd.

Tinbergen, N. 1951, *The Study of Instinct*. Oxford: Oxford University Press.

Waddington, C. H. 1957, *The Strategy of the Genes*. London: George Allen and Unwin Ltd.

Waldeyer-Hartz, H. W. G. von 1891, Über einige neuer Forschungen in Gebiete der Anatomie des Central Nerven Systems, *Berlin Klin. Wschr.*, 28: 691.

Walter, W. G. 1973, Human frontal lobe functions in sensory motor association, *Psychophysiology of the Frontal Lobes*, K. H. Pribram and A. R. Luria (eds.). New York: Academic Press.

Weiskrantz, L., Warrington, E. K., Sanders, M. D. and Marshall, J. 1974, Visual capacity in the hemianopic field following a restricted occipital ablation, *Brain*, 97 (4): 709–28.

Weiss, P. 1952, Central vs peripheral factors in the development of co-ordination, *Res. Publ. Ass. Nerv. Ment. Dis.*, vol. 20, Chap. 1.

Werner, H. and Wapner, S. 1952, Toward a general theory of perception, *Psychol. Rev.*, 59: 324–38.

Wiener, N. 1948, *Cybernetics*. New York: John Wiley & Sons.

Young, J. Z. 1956(a), Growth changes in the diameter of peripheral nerve fibres in fishes, *J. Anat.*, 1: 1–14.

Young, J. Z. 1956(b), Some characteristics of myelinated fibre populations, *J. Anat.*, 2: 172–87.

INDEX

INDEX

Compiled by Betty Dewhurst

Italicized numerals refer to information given in the diagrams.